I0615887

BOOKS

Regional Publishing, National Voice
A division of Philadelphia Stories

93 Old York Road, Ste. 1-753
Jenkintown, PA 19046
www.psbookspublishing.org

© 2016, Philadelphia Stories

Published by PS Books, a divison of Philadelphia Stories, Inc.
All rights reserved.

ISBN 978-0-9904715-4-7

*No part of this book may be reproduced or transmitted in any form
or by any means, electronic or mechanical, including photocopying or
recording, or by any information storage and retrieval system without
permission in writing from the publisher.*

All proceeds from the sale of this book support
Philadelphia Stories, a free nonprofit literary
magazine publishing writers and artists from
the Delaware Valley.

Cover Image: Susan DiGironimo, © 2015

contents

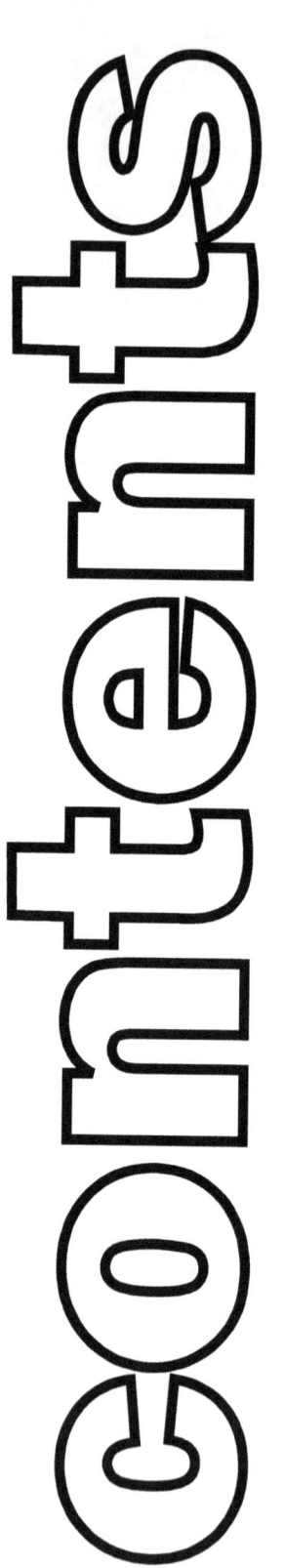

Creative Nonfiction

Short Stories

Flash Fiction

Novel Excerpts

Poetry

Introduction

Grouping artists by any arbitrary criterion is, well, arbitrary. So you might well ask, why bother? And this is a good question. Every time I see a list like the National Book Award's "5 Under 35," or Buzzfeed's "20 Under 40" I can't help but feel a certain amount of resentment. Not that these writers aren't all wonderful and deserving of accolades and praise, but why the special recognition for what some consider a young writer? Combine these ageist notions with the troubling publishing statics for women provided each year by VIDA: Women in the Literary Arts, and my thinking was, it's time to celebrate women authors who aren't necessarily going to be included on these other lists. What is disturbing about these lists is that they place an expiration date on emergence, as if the struggle to publish ends at 40 or finding and refining one's voice as a writer isn't a life long journey.

Some of the writers featured in this anthology are quite well known and others are definitely what most publishers would consider emerging. Some of the works have been published before and others are brand new in print. Many of these authors have won prestigious prizes like the Pushcart, while others have been writing in relative obscurity. I say relative because truthfully, most writers work in obscurity, whether they've won a Pushcart or not. PS Books is proud to continue the work we began in *Extraordinary Gifts: Remarkable Women of the Delaware Valley* by showcasing female writers and artists. These 50 pieces were selected from hundreds of submissions from women across the country (and Canada and Ireland). It would be wonderful if we lived in a world where singling out under-recognized groups wasn't necessary. Wouldn't it be great if we could just pick up a piece of writing and not have to worry about putting the author in a box in order to ensure that all our voices are heard and acknowledged? But for now, this is the world we live in. Acknowledgement matters.

We hope you enjoy this collection of poetry, essays, and fiction from 50 wonderful writers.

Carla Spataro
Editorial Director, PS Books

The Year Hits Perimenopause
Susan Blackwell Ramsey

Autumn has decided what the hell.
She knows the symptoms and already frost
has tarnished her. She's not a fool. She knows
however much she feels like May the snows
are coming, so before this chance is lost
she's going to wear red, show off her tits,
plump apples, bulge pumpkins. She is going to swell
each bunch of grapes to cleavage and shadowed musk.
Fuck decorum, honey, take a bite.
Take two. Each day is shorter than the last
and colder, so her unimpeachable night
is thick with glitter, rhinestones, sequins, glitz.
She thinks that maybe she'll even try her luck
and use her license for a few young bucks.

Susan Blackwell Ramsey's work has appeared in journals ranging from *Poetry Motel* to *The Indiana Review*, *Prairie Schooner*, and *The Southern Review*, and in such anthologies as *The Muse Strikes Back* (Storyline Press,) *Michigan in Poetry, Poetry in Michigan* (New Issues Press), and *Saint Peter's B-List* (Ave Maria Press); her book, *A Mind Like This*, won the 2011 Prairie Schooner Book Prize. She got her BA from Kalamazoo College in 1972 and never really got away again, for years teaching spinning, knitting, and creative writing at the Kalamazoo Institute of Arts. She eventually got an MFA from and taught at the University of Notre Dame, but she still can't seem to stop double-spacing after sentences.

2
My Mother and Father
Eileen Moeller

at the kitchen table,
in a cloud of cigarette smoke,
unable to look each other in the eye.

Neither one moves much,
beyond the occasional lift of
hand to mouth, the draw of lips
on a filter tip, a tap on
the edge of the ashtray.

So two lives fill up;
ashes enough to paint
their faces on Jupiter,
cigarette butts that go on
to infinity, the two of them
spreading out, huge enough
to exhale galaxies.

They are caught in
a huge gravity field,
their marriage bed,
a black hole forcing
them to stay together,
swallowing all they
have left of yes.

The stillness I witness,
like the night sky's,
is deceptive.

The forces of time and
history are moving them,
fast as two comets,
toward early demise.

So much of my life
lived without them.
Two distant astral bodies
that call me into the dark.

Eileen Moeller lives in Medford Lakes, NJ. She has an MA in Creative Writing from Syracuse University, where she taught for many years in the SU Writing Program, as well as at Hamilton College, and at Pratt MWPI. Her poems have appeared in literary journals, including *Ars Medica, Feminist Studies, Paterson Literary Review, Blue Fifth Review, Schuylkill Valley Journal,* and *Philadelphia Stories,* and in anthologies: *Paterson: A Poet's City, Women. Period, Cries of the Spirit: A Celebration of Women's Spirituality, Claiming the Spirit Within: A Sourcebook of Women's Poetry.* She has been the recipient of the Dorothy Damon and Allen Ginsberg awards. Her first book, *Firefly, Brightly Burning,* was published in June by Grayson Books. Access her blog: *And So I Sing: Poems and Iconography,* online.

Albee
Anne Converse Willkomm

Albee got up every day and brushed his teeth, just like Brian had showed him. Then he got dressed: first he put on his socks, then his underpants. His shirt went on next, then his pants. His belt. He couldn't forget his belt. It was leather and had his name painted on it – A-L-B-E-E – in big blue letters. Some of the paint had worn off a little, but that was okay cause he knew how to spell his name. He pulled his pants up high, and then tightened his belt – that way his pants wouldn't fall down, like Mr. Thompson's at the bookstore.

Like every other day, before breakfast he swept or shoveled the sidewalk in front of Jameson's. But today was different; today was the Christmas tree lighting ceremony. It was kind of like summer when there were lots of cars and lots of people on the sidewalks.

"Good morning Albee," Lisa said. "Excited?" she asked, as she put down a plate of fried eggs, bacon – nice and crispy the way Albee liked it, and a cup of coffee. "Sure I can't get you some fruit?"

He shook his head, shoving a forkful of eggs into his mouth.

"We're kind a busy this morning, so come find me if you need more coffee."

"Okay," Albee said.

He swung his feet back and forth scuffing them on the worn wooden floor trying to finish his breakfast as fast as he could. Usually he had two cups of coffee, black with one sugar. Brian had told him once, "Don't have too much sugar, it's bad for your teeth." So Albee did what Brian said and only used one packet. Even though he liked looking at Lisa's packets of sugar because they had pictures of different kinds boats on them – and, sometimes boats like that would come up the river—today he didn't have time to sort the packets or have a second cup of coffee. No, today he had a job to do.

Just like every other day, Albee took his plate and coffee cup into the kitchen. "Hey there, Albee," Frank, the big, tall cook said. He wore shorts even in the winter.

But since today wasn't like every other day, Albee didn't stand and talk with Frank. "Got to go."

"Big day, huh."

Albee nodded. Usually he'd tell Frank about the weather, but today he had to hurry, he had to get to the police station before they gave *his* job to someone else, and he had to stop by the Pharmacy to say "good morning" to Brian. Brian didn't live at the pharmacy like him. He had a house on Pearl

Hill. Albee liked Brian's house, and had wanted to live there, but Brian had told him he needed someone to watch over the pharmacy and that Albee would be the best man for the job.

He walked along the side of the brick building and in through the back door – it squeaked which annoyed Brian, but Albee always thought the door was just saying, "Hello." He pushed through the swinging doors into the rear of the store. *Rudolph the Red Nosed Reindeer* was playing, and green and red garland hung from the ceiling. Albee began humming the song as he walked up to the counter and stood there waiting for Brian, who was just hanging up his black telephone.

"Good night sleep, Albee?"

"Uh huh."

"Big day today, huh."

Albee grinned, a toothy wide kind of grin, the kind his mama used to say brought joy to the angels in heaven. He figured now, it made her happy, too.

"Books, I want more books today, too."

"I'll call Mabel and tell her to drop some more off, or I'll go pick them up at lunch."

"I go, later, after."

Brian leaned on the counter. "No Albee, now you remember, Mabel prefers that you, that I, go get them or that she drop them off."

"Why?"

"Well, that's just the way Mabel likes it."

Albee shrugged his shoulders. "Okay."

"Have fun today Albee, and go up and get your scarf, it's going to be cold today."

"No snow."

"I know it's not going to snow, but it's going to get quite cold later on this afternoon."

Albee did as Brian asked and climbed up the creaky steps into his comfy room, wrapped his scarf around his neck, and then climbed back down the steps and out the door.

He took his usual route up Main Street, passed Port O'Hats, Toys in the Attic, Aunt Minnie's Ice Cream Shop, then up Pearl Hill passed Port Bakers, and around the corner by the fire house. Jimmy, the oldest fireman, always waved and yelled, "Mornin'" to Albee. There was one fireman, Greg, he always laughed when Albee walked by, Brian told him that Greg didn't mean nothing by it, he just got a case of the sillies more than most folks.

As he rounded the corner, Albee's heart was pounding wildly inside his chest. He stumbled, tearing his pants. He hoped Brian wouldn't be mad, and brushed his knee off and his widening grin took hold as he pulled the glass door open, and he barely noticed the sharp clink of the dangling bell as it hit the glass.

"Mornin' Albee," Louise said. She had a nice smile. It reminded Albee of his mother. She'd been gone for a while now. He couldn't exactly remember how long ago she'd gone up to heaven to be with Jesus, but it had been a good amount of time, he knew that. He didn't like thinking about that time though, because it made him sad. She just sat in her chair and wouldn't wake up. And the smell was pretty bad, too. And then he'd gone to live at the Pharmacy.

Albee smiled at Louise.

"Have a seat, Bill will be right out."

"Okay," Albee said barely able to contain his smile.

Louise went back to her telephone conversation. "Albee's here, waiting for Bill. Y'know it's his big day. I think he waits all year for this." She smiled at Albee. That's when he remembered to remove his Boston Red Sox cap. Louise had told him a long time ago he had to take his hat off when he went inside a building.

She turned away from Albee and whispered, "We'll get a few calls later this afternoon about the," But Albee had his eye on Bill's door, focused on it, waiting for it to open, not *really* listening Louise's soft voice murmuring in the background. "Crackpot and the loud horn. Really, what's the matter with people?"

Bill's door opened. A tall, very tall man, walked out, with his back to Albee, while Bill leaned against the door jam.

"Hey Albee," Bill said.

"Hi Bill."

The tall man, Hank, turned and looked at Albee.

"Hank, you remember Albee, he's got something very important to do today."

The tall man's eyes began dancing kind of funny, and Albee knew that kind of dancing meant he was nervous, and Albee figured maybe Hank got a special job today, too, just like him.

"Yeah, a great, well, I've got to run." He turned and walked toward the door as if he was in a hurry. "Thanks again Bill, see you later Louise."

"Bye Hank. Come on in Albee."

Clutching his hat, Albee shuffled into Bill's office. Albee was always a little scared in Bill's office because he had lots and lots of pictures of bad guys on his wall. Some had beards, one had an eye patch, and there was a woman who had done something really, really bad, Bill had told him. So, he sat in the chair next to Bill's desk with his back to all the bad people.

"So are you ready?"

Albee nodded.

"Did Lisa make you a good breakfast this morning?" Bill asked as he thinned out his graying moustache with his fingers.

Albee nodded.

"Well good." Bill walked over to a tall black cabinet with drawers and tugged the top one which screeched as he pulled on it. Albee wiggled around in the metal chair, its feet scraping the floor in protest. He wanted to jump up and grab it out of Bill's hand. He could barely sit still. "You know the drill, Officer Albee, right?"

Albee nodded.

"Here Albee, now off you go to walk your beat."

Albee beamed as he took the bright shiny blue horn, put on his Red Sox cap, adjusted his scarf, and walked out of the office, forgetting to say goodbye to Louise.

"Don't use it all up at once," he heard her say.

He squeezed the black button and let out a loud *Bleeeeeeeeeeeep*. Oh, how exciting that noise was. That grin filled his round face. He took a few more steps. *Bleeeeeeeeeeeep*. As he walked by the firehouse, he blew the air horn again, and again as he walked by Port Bakers. He kept pressing the button as he walked down Pearl Hill, passed the Aunt Millie's Ice Cream shop, by Toys in the Attic and by Port O'Hats. People stopped and watched. He knew they were paying attention to Officer Albee. He got stuck behind a clump of people waiting to get into Jameson's. He blew his horn, and they jumped.

"What's that idiot got a horn for?"

"Why's that grown man blowing his horn around town? You'd think one of the town cops would do something about it."

Didn't they know he was Honery Policeman, Officer Albee? Surely they knew that. He brushed passed them and blew his horn again. He continued blowing his horn as he walked over the bridge and passed the Clam Shack, which was boarded up and closed for the winter. When he reached Walker's Corners, breaks screeched, cars stopped and people began yelling, so he continued blasting his horn, and there was more yelling, and people began using bad words as they pointed at him.

That's when Bill showed up, his blue lights swirling around as he stepped out of his police car. Walking toward the jumble of cars Bill said, "It's okay folks, calm down."

People were still yelling. Albee blew his horn.

"Albee, can you put the horn down for a moment?"

Albee set it on the ground, his eyes flitting back and forth between Bill and each of the people leaning out of the windows of their fancy cars yelling and pointing, and waving their hands, followed by more yelling.

"What are you gonna do about that freak and his horn. Look what he did."

"Sir, calm down. No damage here, just a little traffic jam, is all."

A woman in a fuzzy red Santa hat leaned out of her window, "This is ridiculous, shouldn't he be in some home?"

"Yeah, what's the freak doing wandering about anyway. Gonna get himself hit by a car or something," yelled a man driving a van full of gray-haired people.

Albee stood there. Had he done something bad? Was Bill mad at him? It was clear these people in the cars were mad at him. He didn't know what to do. He looked back toward the center of town, down at his favorite horn, at Bill, at the yelling people. His heart was banging hard. And Albee knew Bill was now mad at him because he was yelling.

Covering his ears and closing his eyes, Albee began to walk away leaving his horn sitting on the sidewalk. "Yayayayaya," he kept saying over and over to drown out the car horns. And even though he opened his eyes every few steps he still ran right into Brian.

"Albee are you okay?" asked Brian as he pulled Albee's hands away from his ears.

"Bill's mad, he's mad at me."

"No Albee, Bill's not mad at you. There was just a lot of confusion. Here, I'll walk you back to Jameson's, it's almost lunchtime."

"No."

"You need to eat."

Albee shook his head because Bill usually had lunch at Jameson's as well, and Albee didn't want to see Bill's mad face.

Freckles, Mrs. Hunter's little white dog stopped to sniff Albee. Mrs. Hunter owned the gift shop around the corner from the pharmacy. She stopped and adjusted the leash in her gloved hand.

"You know Brian, you need to make sure you watch over him, that was quite a mess back there. I mean you have to, well what if –"

"Janet, I assure you, I've got everything under control."

"Well I certainly hope so, that could have been disastrous. Come on Freckles, we need to get back to the store."

Brian let Mrs. Hunter pass then said, "If you don't want to go and sit at Lisa's, then I'll bring you up a sandwich."

Albee and Brian separated. Brian continued down the sidewalk toward Jameson's while Albee crossed the street, walking along the side of the pharmacy. Freckles who was now tied to the bench next to the door of the gift shop, barked at Albee, and on any other day, Albee might have spoken to the dog, because they were friends, but today he walked in through the back door, up the noisy stairs, and plopped himself onto his bed.

A new pile of picture books sat on the edge of his red and blue quilt. The top one was red and it had a picture of that scary fuzzy thing. Brian loved to read the book about the Grinch, but it wasn't one of Albee's favorites. He set the book back on top of the pile.

Brian returned with a peanut butter and jelly sandwich and sat down on the side of Albee's bed. "You have to forget about those people in their cars. They aren't from around here, they just come to our small town to visit the pretty shops, see our lobster pot-decorated tree, and eat our terrific food. What's unfortunate is that we *need* them. I know that's hard for you to understand."

Albee kept looking at the floor.

Brian patted Albee on the back. "All you need to know is that I will always take care of you. You're like family to me."

"Like Rita and Matty?" Now Brian looked down at the floor. "You still sad bout them?" Albee asked.

Bill sighed. "Just miss them, probably like you miss your mother."

"Love you Brian."

"Albee, I love you too. I always will. Forget about those folks. Why don't you look at the books Mable dropped off, and then draw, or watch television. You're gonna want your rest before the tree lighting tonight."

* * * * *

Albee got up everyday and brushed his teeth, just like Brian had showed him. After getting dressed, he swept the sidewalk in front of Jameson's before going in for breakfast. And today was no different. He grabbed the broom from behind the door and swept the sidewalk, and he wondered when there would be some snow to sweep or shovel?

He ate his breakfast, fried eggs, and bacon – nice and crispy, just the way he liked it. Lisa had forgotten to ask him about the fruit, and that made him happy – she was very busy. Albee knew there were two times a year when the town was busy, summer time and right before Christmas. Lisa even forgot his second cup of coffee, but that was okay.

The radio in the kitchen was loud and the dishwasher and prep cook were singing a song that Albee didn't recognize.

"Christmas music," he said to no one in particular when he took his plate in through the swinging doors.

"What you mumblin' about?" said the Jerry, the dishwasher, a short fella who always wore a blue bandana, as he walked toward Albee wiping his hands on his dirty apron, getting taller and taller the closer he got.

"Hey, leave him alone Jerry," said Frank. "So any snow in the forecast, Albee?"

Albee shook his head.

"Oh well, Mother Nature will unleash her fury when she's good and ready, and not a minute before."

Albee stared at Frank; he wasn't exactly sure what he'd just said, so he smiled. He'd learned that's what people do when they got nothing to say, kind of like saying 'Hello' without any words. Yes, Albee had learned that a long time ago.

"Time for my walk."

"Okay, you enjoy now."

Albee nodded and walked out of Jameson's. He looked up at the blue sky, no snow today, he thought. He walked along the sidewalk, until he was at the crossing place, then crossed and walked into the backdoor of the Village Pharmacy.

Brian was with a customer. Albee thought it was Mr. Noble. Albee waited because he wasn't supposed to go for his walk in the winter without telling Brian first. He waited, and waited, until Mr. Noble stepped away from the counter.

"Hey Albee, off for your morning walk?"

Albee nodded.

"Okay, I'll see you in a little while." And just like every other winter day, Brian looked at his watch.

Albee strolled along the streets and storefronts; some were closed and some just smelled really good, just like Christmas. He waved at almost everyone, some waved back, some were very busy, Albee knew that.

Kids without their winter coats or hats went running by, one of them banged into Albee, thrusting him up against one of the little shops. The kid turned around, "Hey look it's –" and they began laughing. Albee laughed too, even though he wasn't exactly sure what was funny. That's when Mr. Kraus opened his shop door, "You kids get going, you too Albee, move along now."

"Okay, Mr. Kraus," said Albee. He still wanted to know what was funny. He thought maybe kids just laughed a lot, cause kids just did – he knew that.

On his way back into town, Albee looked up at the bookstore. Mr.

Thompson always strung his lights in the big window to look like a gigantic Christmas tree. Mr. Thompson was standing in the window, Albee waved, and Mr. Thompson nodded. He never waved back because he was always holding his pipe with one hand and his belt with the other.

By the time he returned, and it had gotten so cold outside, that he decided to go straight to lunch, where Lisa gave him a bowl of fish chowder and the funny little circle crackers. He always liked two packs.

After lunch, Brian liked Albee to relax in his room and watch television or look at his books. And Albee liked to sit in his warm room and watch television or look at his books. And Mabel had dropped off even more Christmas books.

For dinner, Albee had more fish chowder with two packs of the little circle crackers. But, when Albee asked for a second bowl, Lisa told him they were so busy, she doubted she'd have enough, so instead she brought him some chicken noodle. Albee didn't like chicken noodle. Frank said he wouldn't tell Lisa and brought Albee a bowl of chocolate ice cream with whip cream on the top. Frank called it a mountain of whip cream – it didn't look like a mountain to Albee.

After dinner, Albee went back to his room and Brian would usually come up and they'd play a few hands of Go Fish before Brian left to go to his house. Albee sometimes wondered if Brian's Rita and Matty had met his mama in heaven.

"Okay pal. You beat me three straight hands. I'm beat. You okay?"

Albee nodded.

"Well, you get a good night's sleep, and I'll see you after breakfast tomorrow."

"Okay Brian."

Brian left and Albee turned on his television. He liked to watch Wheel of Fortune before he went to sleep. The spinning wheel was his favorite. And he liked to mimic Pat Sajak: "There must be an 'n,'" or "Yes, there is an 'h.' "Oh boy, I'm sorry, you got it that time." And Albee would continue through each puzzle, "Yes, there is a 'B,' an 's,' an 'l.' You want to guess? Yes, Fresh Blanket of Snow is correct." Albee especially liked the $5000 spot on the wheel, it sparkled and the contestants jumped up and down and screamed if they landed on it.

After Wheel of Fortune Albee turned out his light and went to sleep.

* * * * *

Albee got up everyday and brushed his teeth, just like Brian had showed him. After getting dressed, he swept the sidewalk in front of Jameson's before going in for breakfast. And today was no different, except that he had to sweep a fresh layer of snow. He loved snow. He'd been waiting for snow. It was so pretty with all the white twinkling lights in the store windows. It made him think about *his* Christmas tree.

He didn't have a tree in his room. No, his tree was at Jameson's near the cash machine. It was Christmas Eve and there were so many presents with shiny bows under the tree and lots and lots of dollar bills taped to the branches. Albee loved his tree. It had colored lights and red balls. Every year Frank would help him climb up on the stepladder and put the shiny silver star on the tippy-top. Then on Christmas Eve, he got to open the presents and Brian got the dollar bills.

He was sitting near the kitchen eating his breakfast, fried eggs, and bacon – nice and crispy, just the way he liked it. His coffee seemed extra hot, so he blew on it and waited until it cooled. Folks were walking in rubbing their hands together, and talking about the cold weather. Didn't they know it was winter? Winter was always cold.

Frank stepped out of the kitchen wiping his hands on his not-so-white apron and then sat down with Albee. "So, Albee it's Christmas Eve."

Albee nodded his head. And Lisa walked over with the steaming coffee pot in her hand and sat down in the chair at the next table.

"I think we need to find a different place for you to have dinner tonight," Lisa said.

"Brian, I have it with Brian. Always the same." Looking away from Frank, Albee carefully flicked the strawberry off his plate. Every so often Lisa tucked one or two in along side his bacon, but he didn't like strawberries.

"Well, Brian ain't feeling too well. They had to take him to the hospital last night. That's why Mr. Gardener is at the Pharmacy this morning," Frank said.

Albee looked up at Frank. He didn't like what Frank was saying, no he did not like it one bit.

"Can he go to your house?" Lisa asked.

"No, I'm going to my girlfriends and she don't understand, you know. Can't he go to yours?"

"No, I'm having my entire family at my house tonight," Lisa said and then looked at Albee. "We'll find some place else for you to go." Looking back at Frank, "I'm swamped here, we've never been so busy. And I still have Christmas shopping to do."

"Don't you think Brian must have had some sort of contingency plan?" Frank asked. Albee wasn't sure what that big word meant.

"He must have, he of all people, knows things just happen. Bill might know. We'll have to call Bill later," Lisa said. "Cause someone's got to take him."

"Okay," said Frank, then looking at Albee he added, "One of us will call Bill later." Frank got up, wiped his hands on his apron and walked back into the kitchen whistling, *All I Want for Christmas is My Two Front Teeth.*

Albee didn't want to go to anyone else's house for Christmas Eve dinner – he always spent it with Brian. And he was still going to spend it with Brian. He got up and walked out of Jameson's, leaving his plate and coffee cup in the table. He rushed across the street, slipping in the snow, and eventually falling as he tried to round the corner to the side of the Village Pharmacy. He wanted to cry, his knee hurt, but he had to find Brian.

He walked in through the back door, but instead of going up the noisy stairs to his room, he slipped into the back door. Mr. Gardener was standing there behind the counter. He didn't like Mr. Gardener; he wasn't mean or nothing, just not like Brian. He stood there and waited.

"Not now Albee, I'm busy. Just go up to your room, I'll come find you later."

Albee sat on his bed and he waited and he waited, but Mr. Gardener didn't come. He looked around the room, tried to look at one of his picture books, but he couldn't, it didn't seem right. Then he remembered when he'd been real sick one time, Brian had sat next to his bed all day and all night. And he thought he remembered his mama doing that, too. And then he remembered the day his mama didn't wake up. He hadn't been home because his mama had sent him off for the day to help plant flowers at church. Sitting there, he wondered if he hadn't gone to plant the flowers if she still would have fallen asleep. He had to go sit with Brian. He had to make sure Brian woke up.

He wasn't sure exactly where the hospital was, but he remembered seeing the ambulance always going out by the savings bank. Putting on his coat and his Red Sox cap, he looked around the small room for the mittens Mabel had made him. One of the thumbs had a hole it in, but he loved them because they were his favorite color, blue. Mabel knit him a new pair every Christmas – always blue. They had fallen on the floor.

He poked his head in to tell Mr. Gardener where he was going, but he was with a customer, and he didn't want to get yelled at again.

The wind was strong and the snow that had fallen the night before was blowing around. Albee walked down Church Street by the savings bank toward the school. He had always wanted to go to school, but his mama had told him school was not the right place for him. School kids were mean. He wasn't so sure they were mean; they just seemed to laugh a lot.

In the dusky light, more snow began to fall and the wind burned his cheeks, but he kept on walking. Beyond the school, the street was unfamiliar. Open snow covered fields took over, and the sidewalk stopped. Brian had told him, never to walk in the street unless it was an emergency, and this seemed like an emergency.

Brian needed him, and he needed Brian.

Albee kept walking even though he was very cold. What seemed odd was that his feet didn't really feel cold any more, he couldn't really feel them at all – same with his fingers and his nose. The snow was getting deeper and it was now dark. He was scared of the dark.

The wind was howling like a wild animal. Albee wondered if wild animals were out in the winter, he hoped not. And he was getting tired. He could see a bench up ahead under a single street light. He'd rest there, just a few minutes, warm up, and then be able to find the hospital, find Brian.

When he got to the bench, he decided to keep going because the bench was in front of a graveyard. He was definitely scared of graveyards – ghosts and terrible things lived in graveyards. Pete the gasman had told him that once. So Albee kept on walking until he could walk no more and sat with his back against the trunk of a tall pine, pulled his knees up close and watched the tiny flakes of snow as they landed on his nose. He remembered seeing snowflakes in a book once – how pretty they were, all different, and as he closed his eyes he imagined them big, just like in the book.

Anne Converse Willkomm received her AB from Bowdoin College and her MFA in creative writing from Rosemont College, where she is the Director of the Graduate Publishing Programs and also teaches composition and creative writing in the undergraduate college. Prior to her tenure at Rosemont, Anne worked as a freelance editor/writer, working on projects ranging from grants, brochures, press releases, and books. Her creative work has been published in *The Medulla Review, Postcard Shorts, Fiction365, Sybil Magazine, FlashFiction.net, The Midwest Coast Review,* and the anthology "Memoirs of Meanness." Her longer works of fiction were twice named semi-finalists in the William Faulkner Creative Writing Competition.

The Mother As Persephone
Alison Hicks

Call *Mama* into the hole?
Tear at its grassy sides, and finally go home
to the life that began with that opening?
What's a daughter to do.

She can hear her in her head.
She can come back to that meadow.
It makes no difference.
The hole fills in.

A figure who looks like her mother
sits down to table, eats lustily
from her plate, no longer understanding
the distinction between *yours* and *mine*.

When a mother grows crooked, bent,
what can a daughter do,
with no power to trade,
no gift to rescind from the world?

In the meadow, wildflowers bloom.
She puts her ear to the ground,
her blood will not open it.
Hades spits on her youth, wants nothing of her offerings.

Her mother has eaten the pomegranate.
With each seed she forgets a little more.

Alison Hicks is the author of a full-length collection of poems, *Kiss* (PS Books, 2011), a chapbook, *Falling Dreams* (Finishing Line Press, 2006), and a novella, *Love: A Story of Images* (AWA Press, 2004), a finalist in the 1999 Quarterly West Novella Competition. Her work has appeared in *Broad River Review*, *Crack the Spine*, *Eclipse*, *Fifth Wednesday*, *Gargoyle*, *Licking River Review*, *The Ledge*, *Louisville Review*, *Muddy River Poetry Review*, *Permafrost*, *Sanskrit*, *Whiskey Island*, and other journals. Awards include the 2011 Philadelphia City Paper Poetry Prize and two Pennsylvania Council on the Arts fellowships. She is founder of Greater Philadelphia Wordshop Studio, which offers community-based writing workshops.

Amen
Megan Vered

I knew that Mom would not linger. My impression is that people die the way they live, and Mom was efficient. I called my siblings and all the grandchildren that lived nearby. "If you want to say good-bye, go. Now." I called James and told her I could feel Mom leaving, like a tug on my umbilical cord.

"Ahh, Megan, I'm so sorry. Do you want me to come?"

"How could I do this without you?"

"I'll be on the next train."

Relief. I would not be alone.

It was December 27—the day after my birthday and two days after Christmas—the anniversary of my father's death. Mom had recently told the nurse, "It's been almost thirty years. I really miss my husband, you know."

When I arrived at the skilled nursing facility, Mom was surrounded by grown grandchildren. They soothed and stroked her, as she had done for them so many times in the past. Tiny in the huge hospital bed, I could feel her soaking in their love with her eyes.

Soon we heard a light knock on the door. James entered, wearing a dark green suit, dressed like she was going to church. She held me close, pressed her lips to my cheek. She stood over Mom's frail body, held her hand. "Mrs. Hesterman, you are one of my best friends." She pulled Mom's favorite reading chair to the head of the bed, draped herself with a blanket, and remained by my mother's side until morning. I knew she was praying, and after all we'd been through together, it was perfectly reasonable to have Jesus in the room with us.

* * * * *

When I was young, my mother—a first-generation American Jew bruised by the Holocaust—often said, "I wouldn't trust that person to hide me in her closet." Raised in Boston in the Jewish ghetto, she was leery of gentiles and extremely offended when a Christian woman in our neighborhood sent a converted Jew to visit, in the hopes that Mom would accept Jesus as her savior. Jesus did not have a seat at my family table. Not until James Ella arrived. James was raised in Alabama by her Baptist grandmother. Her most-common utterance was, "In the name of Jesus, amen."

I met James when I was five. The first thing I noticed when she walked through the front door was how tall she was next to my diminutive mother.

Her face was expressive, the kind that could tell stories. She stooped down until our eyes matched. "Hi, I'm James."

I held tightly to the pleat of my mother's skirt, worrying the dense fabric between tiny fingers. "James—that's a funny name for a girl." In my mind I pictured a boy in my kindergarten class we called Jimmy, whose real name was James.

"You're right about that."

When she smiled, I could almost count her beautiful white teeth. Now that she was up close, I noticed the scar that cut across her forehead, past her eyebrow, and down into her cheek. I remembered I hadn't introduced myself. "I'm Megan. It's a funny name too, but more like a girl than yours."

Mom and James laughed, I supposed because of what I said, though I didn't think I'd said anything funny.

Eve came up from the basement playroom, thumb in mouth, stuffed bunny in tow. James bent down to say hello, and then Eve was up above me in James's arms, bunny ears flopping. I was normally the one who threw myself into strangers' arms, but not this time. Even though this one appeared beautiful and friendly, I decided I would keep an eye on her.

It was the end of summer, and we'd just returned from our family camping trip to Sand Pond. Hours on the beach, tumbling in and out of cool green water, rolling in the coarse sand, playing hide-and-seek in the trees. Back home with the dust of the Sierras ground into our pores, pine needles stuck to our hair, and a mountain of laundry by the washing machine.

My father came home from collecting rent at one of the apartment buildings he owned in Oakland to find my mother elbow-deep in dirty clothes. She normally had a housekeeper to help her, but the most recent one had vanished.

"I need help!" Mom cried.

My father replied, "There's this one woman I've seen. Her apartment is immaculate every time I go there. I think she's looking for work."

"Bring her to me! Now!"

Dad and his driver, Lemuel, took off and before long, returned to the house with James. She tackled that mountain of laundry—which was just the beginning—and stayed with us for the next twelve years. After she arrived, I could feel my mother relax, like James was the one she'd been waiting for all along. From that day on, Mom—even though she didn't believe in God—described James as a godsend, and even though she didn't trust gentiles, she entrusted James with the care of what mattered most to her in the world: her family and her home.

I was understandably leery after the parade of housekeepers that had come and gone. The first one I remember came when I was three. Black hair slicked back into a bun on the top of her head. So tight it made her eyes stretch. When making beds, she would hold the feathery pillow between stubby white teeth and shimmy the pillowcase up toward her nose, making her stout tummy, hips, and bosom shake. She called us "hammerheads." Every day she yelled, "Come here, hammerhead! Stop that, hammerhead!" She was so mean, my mother made her leave. After her, we had one with slim long arms, fair skin, and sleek red-toned hair. Even though she wore a white uniform and shoes with thick white laces, Mom told me she showed up for work drunk one morning, and that was the end of her.

It was not long before James took on the role of second mother. She brought a traditional sense of discipline into the house, trying her best to tame the chaos engendered by my father's shifty business schemes, wild older brothers, and a general sense of laissez-faire circulating in the house. My mother, who initially wanted nine children, assumed we would be cut from her compliant, rule-following cloth, only to be surprised by a flock of hellions. While she took to her bed—the only quiet place in the house—with migraines, James chased my brothers, sent all five of us to our rooms, forced us to apologize to each other and to her. She even washed my brother Oran's mouth out with soap after he called her a bitch under his breath, claiming all the way to the bathroom, "I said witch! I said witch!"

James never had children and it was not long before we heard that the people in her church were referring to us as her "white family." Differences aside, she and my mother shared an intuitive understanding about mothering. They formed a partnership in which words were never exchanged. James struggled to manage our mouthy, disrespectful behavior, and years later told me she prayed every day she would live long enough to see how we turned out.

James was the first person who ever prayed in our house; she relied on the Lord for all requests. My mother, who did not believe in prayer, began to say things like, "It must be so comforting for her to have something to believe in." My father, an agnostic, made a joke of it by saying, "I wasn't expecting so much Jesus in our house."

James brought a new moral standard to our home, where truth was often as slippery as black ice. She never lied. Even if she cheated at solitaire, she'd say, "I won with two cheats."

When Mom and Dad went out of town on business trips, James often spoiled us with homemade fried chicken (Mom did not allow fried food in the house) and fresh fruit cobbler, with a dash of Christian prayer. We said grace before meals, kneeled by our beds at night, even went to church with her on Sunday mornings. The only white faces amid dramatic falling-out episodes and cries of *Amen* and *Praise the Lord*. Her resolute belief in something larger than herself intrigued me, and I paid close attention when she and my grandmother, a staunch Zionist and nonbeliever, argued about the existence of God while playing gin rummy. This was in stark contrast to my parents, who avoided religious discussions with James. Curiously, they set no limits on her expressions of devotion.

I didn't go to James's house until I was much older, but I knew a lot about her. She had beautiful swirly handwriting. She always wore a pretty, perfectly fitted dress under her apron. She went to church at least twice a week and read the Bible every day. She was married when she first came to work for us and then got divorced. She was a very intent listener. When she laughed at a funny story, her eyes filled with tears.

* * * * *

James and I sat vigil by my mother's bedside. For twelve hours she lay between life and death, eyes closed. I paid close attention to her labored breathing. Mom had witnessed my first breath, and I was soon to witness her last. I sang lullabies and did my best to help her. I reminded her throughout the night that my father, her parents, and her siblings were on the other side, waiting. James—who had been my mother's rock through countless family celebrations as well as upsets—offered a steady presence.

* * * * *

I phoned my sister to tell her that Mom was gone. James, who after all these years was still unable to use my mother's first name, wiped tears and said, "Mrs. Hesterman, you were my best friend. You were always the same."

We sat quietly with Mom's body, and James began to reminisce. She told me about an interaction I did not remember, that we'd had when I was in elementary school. She'd just come up from doing the ironing and watching her afternoon stories: *All My Children, The Guiding Light, As the World Turns.* I rushed through the front door and flung my sweater across the living room sofa. She asked me to pick it up. I ignored her.

Exasperated, she said, "I don't know where your mother got you from."

"I came out of my mother's stomach!" I said with know-it-all defiance.

"Too bad she can't put you back in," she said.

"You're not even part of this family!" I yelled.

Pausing to touch the blanket covering my mother's body, she told me that was the one time her feelings got hurt. "I guess somehow I'd got to thinking that I was a member of the family. But you sure set me straight."

Mortified to hear that I had ever hurt her feelings, I apologized. James had been there for all of the milestones in my life; we'd been intertwined for years. "When I look at you, I see myself. You are my family, my genetic material."

Her eyes brightened.

"Anyway, you are my mother now. Whether you like it or not. And don't even think about dying. I'm putting you on death restriction."

In the name of Jesus.

Amen.

Megan Vered, an MFA candidate at Vermont College of Fine Arts, lived on a kibbutz at age 18, roasted her first turkey (giblets and all) at 20, had her first child at 26, and published her first essay at 48. She is a 10-year cancer survivor and lived through 9 Minnesota winters. Her publication credits include: *The San Francisco Chronicle, Amarillo Bay, Existere Journal of Arts and Literature, The Oklahoma Review, The Penman Review, Lake Effect*. A featured essayist for *Mezzo Cammin*, Megan is also the co-host of Say The Word, a reading series in San Francisco.

Casting the First Stone
Lisa Lawmaster Hess

CHAPTER ONE

Marita Mercer adjusted the icicle-thin strap of her leopard print camisole, and then tugged once, twice, three times. Perfect. Enough cleavage to look casually sexy, but not so much that Jim could brand her a wanton woman unworthy of her own daughter.

"Mom, do you have to wear that?" Twelve-year-old Charli flopped onto Marita's bed. "Isn't it bad enough that dad's dragging us through this mediation? Are you trying to make it easy for him to win?"

"Of course not. Besides, you'll barely see it." Marita slipped a black jacket on over the camisole. "See? A sensible black suit. Sober and appropriate for all proceedings."

"Didn't you wear that to work yesterday?"

"As a matter of fact, I did. But yesterday, this suit was a uniform for a court reporter. Today, it's outward proof that I can be boring and follow the rules."

Charli sighed. "Maybe we should just take Grandma and Grandpa up on their offer. If I transfer to Holy Redeemer, maybe Dad and Angel will lay off."

Marita sat down beside her daughter. "Do you really want to go to Christian school?"

"No. But I don't want to live with Dad and Angel either."

"Honey, your father and Angel won't necessarily back off just because I send you to Holy Redeemer. They want full custody. Anyway, your father could easily argue that Holy Redeemer didn't do much for me."

Charli laughed. "I still can't believe you went there for twelve years."

Eleven, Marita refused to voice aloud, remembering how everyone—the teachers, the principal, her parents—had insisted that she "find a more appropriate educational placement" when they'd found out she was pregnant. Get thee to a nunnery indeed. "Yeah, I'm hardly the poster child for Christian education. And it's a good thing, too. Somebody has to let you have some fun." She stood and selected a pair of thin, gold hoops from the jewelry box on her dresser, then turned back to her daughter. "Why don't you go ahead downstairs? I'll be there in a minute."

"Okay. But hurry. We don't want to be late." Charli slid off the bed and bounded out of the bedroom, her brown ponytail bobbing up and down.

Running a hand through her own thick, dark hair, Marita turned back to the mirror mounted above her dresser. Nearly thirteen years had passed since she'd met Jim Alessio at that Chi Phi party. Her hair had been the same color as Charli's then, with no need for purchased highlights to hide the grey that had begun encroaching even before her thirtieth birthday.

At nineteen, Jim had been older, charming, and just what Marita needed to show her parents that there was more to life than youth group and Sunday services. She'd planned to sneak out, have some fun, rebel a little. She hadn't planned on Charli.

"Mom!" Charli called. "Are you coming?"

Marita slipped a thin gold bangle on her right wrist and pulled her watch onto her left. "Be right there!"

Jim hadn't wanted Charli when she was born. There was no way Marita was letting him have her now.

* * * * *

Angel Alessio pulled her feet out of the stirrups and sat up, her paper gown rustling.

"Is everything okay?" she asked.

"Perfectly fine," Dr. Harrison said, rinsing the speculum and setting it on a paper towel. "I can't see any reason why you and your husband would have trouble conceiving. How long have you been trying?"

"Six months." Angel bit her lip as tears welled in her eyes.

"I know this is difficult," Dr. Harrison said. "But you're young and healthy, and even though six months feels like a long time, it's not uncommon for couples to take twice as long as that to conceive, particularly if the woman has been on the Pill."

"But I've never been on the Pill," Angel said. "I don't believe in contraception."

"Then it's probably just a matter of time." Dr. Harrison made a note in Angel's chart. "In the meantime, try to relax. Stress can inhibit conception."

Great. "Should I plan on seeing an infertility specialist?"

Dr. Harrison flipped her chart closed. "We don't have any reason to believe you're infertile, Mrs. Alessio."

"Well, I mean, isn't it difficult to get an appointment? If I call now—"

"It's too soon. You haven't been trying long enough to be classified as infertile." Dr. Harrison smiled. "This is supposed to be fun, remember?"

"That's what my husband keeps saying. I just never imagined it would be this difficult."

Dr. Harrison patted Angel's hand. "I know. But we have every reason to believe that the next time I see you, you'll be pregnant. Take care."

As soon as Dr. Harrison shut the door, Angel took a deep breath and slid off the table. She crossed to the dressing area in three long strides, fighting back tears. She was relieved that everything was normal, of course—just as Jim had said it would be—but if that were true, then why wasn't she pregnant? She knew women who had gotten pregnant on their honeymoons, others who'd conceived second children while still nursing the first, and yet six months of trying had gotten her nothing but disappointment and a sense of utter failure.

And then there was Marita. She and Jim had been together only once, and that was all it had taken for Marita to get what she hadn't wanted—what Angel now wanted more than anything else in the world.

Angel slipped her flowery pink dress on over her head and tightened the matching belt to the fourth notch, wondering once again if she should have worn something more business-like instead. But Jim had told her to be herself, so she had worn her favorite spring dress, hoping it would bring her good news, or at least some semblance of comfort. So far, it had brought her neither.

At the front desk, Angel made small talk with the receptionist and signed her check with a flourish, making sure to put the little heart over the "i" in Alessio. Sliding her checkbook into the appropriate compartment in her purse, she sailed through the waiting area and out the front doors, burying her disappointment beneath a practiced veneer of sunshine. No need to let everyone in the waiting room know that she was upset.

Once in the car, Angel checked the dashboard clock. Just enough time to make it to the courthouse. It was a good thing she and Jim had taken separate cars.

To go with their separate ideas.

Angel shook her head, trying to shake off the unwanted thought. She was Jim's wife. It was her job to support him. And Charli was Jim's daughter. It was natural for a father to want to play an active role in his child's life. His desire to pursue full custody had nothing to do with the fact that she couldn't seem to get pregnant. *Did it?*

Angel bit her lip. She had no time for tears. It took thirteen minutes to get to the courthouse and she had only fifteen.

Maybe she should call Jim. She pulled her cell phone out of her bag and tapped the screen.

Jim picked up on the first ring. "Where are you?"

Angel took a quick breath, pushing back the ubiquitous tears. "Just leaving the doctor's office."

"Cutting it kind of close, aren't you?"

Angel checked her rearview mirror and put the car in reverse. "Sorry. Dr.

Harrison was running a little behind."

"Well, let's just hope the mediator is, too. Park in the garage on Main—no sense wasting time circling the courthouse, looking for a spot."

Angel pulled out of the parking lot and onto the street. "Okay." *Don't you even want to know how my appointment went?*

"See you soon."

Angel took another deep breath, set her cell phone in its holder on the dashboard, and stopped at a red light. The engine hummed quietly, but did little to drown out the echo of the thoughts she wanted so desperately to set aside.

She turned on the radio. Maybe it was better that Jim hadn't asked about her appointment with Dr. Harrison. Rehashing it would just intensify the pain.

Steeling herself for what was to come, she turned left on Market, praying that the mediator wouldn't ask her to speak.

* * * * *

"Charli, stop."

Charli pulled her thumbnail out of her mouth and stuffed her hand in her pocket. "Sorry, Mom."

"You've been biting your nails since we walked into the courthouse. Why don't you go to the vending machine and get some gum? Or a bottle of juice?"

Charli stood up and took the two dollars Marita held out. "Mom? What if the mediator says I have to live with Dad and Angel?"

"She's not going to."

"How do you know?"

Marita sighed. "I don't. I just—"

The elevator chimed and opened its doors. Charli's father stepped off the elevator, looking more corporate casual than restaurant sales. Marita took a deep breath and was immediately caught off-guard by the spicy aroma of his expensive cologne, a far cry from the drugstore brand that he'd seemingly bathed in the night they'd met.

At thirty-one, James Francis Patrick Alessio was even more handsome than he'd been at nineteen. Charli had inherited his slim, athletic build, and when Jim stood beside her daughter, Marita couldn't help but notice that they looked like a page torn from a preppy clothing catalog. Jim in his khakis, navy polo shirt, and loafers and Charli in her perfectly faded jeans, white tee shirt, and white sneakers. For one brief moment, as Charli wrapped her arms around her father, Marita wondered if she was being unfair—if maybe Charli belonged with Jim. Then a wave of nausea crashed over Marita at the sight of this man who threatened to take away the only good thing he'd ever done for her.

Over my dead body.

Charli pulled out of the hug and glanced nervously from her mother to her father. "I was just going to get some juice," she said. "But I could wait here with you guys instead."

Marita pasted on a smile designed to mask her malice toward Charli's father. "We'll be fine, honey. Go ahead and get your juice."

"Okay. Does anyone want anything?"

Just for this whole nightmare to be over. "Nothing for me, thanks."

"Nor me," Jim said. "But don't dawdle. We don't want to keep the mediator waiting. That doesn't make a good impression."

"Oh," Charli said, panic in her eyes. "Should I stay here?"

"No, honey, you'll be fine." Marita bit her lip. *Why did he feel the need to make Charli more nervous than she already was?*

"Okay. I'll be quick." Charli started down the hall at a brisk pace, and Marita watched her until she knew she was out of earshot.

"Can't you see how worried she is? Do you have to make it worse?"

Jim shrugged. "Punctuality is an important life skill, Marita. One our daughter will learn once she comes to live with me. Along with dressing appropriately."

"She looks fine," Marita said, pushing aside the pang of guilt that stabbed through her as she realized she'd worried more about her own outfit than Charli's. Regaining her composure, she made a show of looking at her watch. "Evidently punctuality is a skill your wife hasn't yet mastered. Perhaps she prefers a dramatic entrance."

Jim gave her his salesman smile, but his clenched jaw told Marita she'd hit the mark. "For your information, she had a doctor's appointment. I expect her momentarily."

"I suppose psychoanalysis is an inevitable part of being married to you. Thank God I didn't succumb."

"I don't recall asking you."

Marita glanced down the hallway again, making sure Charli was still out of earshot. "You don't recall a lot of things. Like the fact that you never wanted Charli in the first place."

"Marita, I was in no position to take on the responsibility of raising a child. Fortunately, my circumstances have changed."

"Yeah. Now you have a deluded little wife just dying to play mommy, allowing you the luxury of looking like you're doing the right thing when, in fact, nothing has changed at all."

The elevator chimed again, and its doors opened, releasing a cloud of expensive floral perfume. As the tiny blonde in the blindingly pink, flowered dress stepped off the elevator, Jim smirked at Marita and tapped the face of his watch.

"Oh, good," Angel said, crossing the lobby to greet her husband. "I'm not late."

Behind Angel, a well-dressed older couple stepped off the elevator and crossed the lobby. Marita's stomach dropped. She glanced down the hall, but it was too late. Her daughter had already seen them.

Charli sprinted down the hall and wrapped her arms around first the man, then the woman. "Grandpa! Grandma! What are you guys doing here?"

Before anyone could reply, the mediator stepped out into the hallway. "Good morning, everyone," she said. "We'll be ready to begin in about ten minutes. Judge Mercer, will you and your wife be joining us?"

"Indeed we will, Jessica," he answered.

"No, Dad," Marita said. "I don't think so."

CHAPTER TWO

Marita clicked her bronze-lacquered nails against the slats of the bench in the courthouse lobby and stared at the closed door of the law library. *Ten minutes.* She had ten minutes to convince her father that she could handle this by herself. Otherwise, he would take over like he always did, hiding his interference in Charli's life behind a smokescreen of legalese and good grooming.

But could she do this alone? This was mediators and courts and lawyers, a system she'd inhabited for years but never fully understood. She had no idea how to find legal representation and mount a battle to keep her daughter. But she had a sneaking suspicion that Jim would be very, very good at it.

Charli plopped down next to Marita on the bench, her juice bottle empty. "Mom, is there a bathroom around here?"

Marita smiled. "You never could hold your juice. Down the hall and on the left, but come right back. We'll be starting soon."

Marita watched her daughter's retreating back then checked her watch. Two minutes before ten. She wanted to leap up off the bench, follow Charli down the hall, and whisk her out a back door, far away from Jim and Angel, from courthouses and mediators.

But if she did, she'd lose everything. Marita might not know what the mediator was going to say, but she'd spent enough time in this building and had seen enough *Lifetime* television movies to know that grabbing Charli and running would only make things worse. Besides, running away would just prove to her parents and Jim and Angel that they were right—that Marita wasn't the one who should be raising Charli, teaching her values and "life skills," or modeling responsibility.

And maybe she wasn't the best role model. But Charli was her daughter, and there was no way she was going to let anyone lead her down some straight and narrow path that excluded any life that didn't meet with their approval.

Marita's father sat down beside her on the bench. "So. Have you come to your senses?"

She sighed. "I really don't know what good it will do if you come in. The mediator has already heard from all of us. She's just giving us her recommendations this morning."

"And while it was a mistake allowing you to have that first meeting without me, I have no intention of compounding it by sending you into that room alone again. If nothing else, my presence here seems to have had an impact on Charli's father."

Marita looked across the waiting area. Jim's complacent smirk was gone, replaced by a plastic smile that barely concealed his scowl. That alone almost made keeping her father here worth it.

"So, I will simply sit quietly at the table and listen."

Marita recognized the tone. The fact that she was a grown woman with a mind—and a child—of her own was immaterial. There was no point in arguing, and even less sense in wasting precious energy on a battle she wouldn't win. "Fine."

Her father patted her hand, sharing his condescension with a mere gesture. "Good choice."

The door to the law library opened, and the mediator came out into the hallway just as Charli returned from the bathroom. "Let's get started."

"Of course," Marita said, pasting on a smile and trying not to grit her teeth.

"Charlotte, why don't you stay out here with me?" Marita's mother said.

"But I—" Charli began.

"That's actually a good idea," Marita said, relieved that she wouldn't have to handle this with Charli in the room. "I'll fill you in afterwards, sweetheart, I promise." Wow. Taking her parents' unsolicited intrusion in stride. She really was desperate.

"Fine." Charli plopped down on the bench and into a slouch that caused Marita's mother to raise her eyebrows.

"Thanks, Mom." Marita turned away from her mother and gave Charli a quick kiss before joining the others in the law library. Her heart was beating furiously and her hands were shaking, so she folded them in her lap to keep them still and out of both her father's line of vision and Jim's.

"Ms. Mercer, Mr. and Mrs. Alessio, you're aware of our previous discussion. Judge Mercer, just to bring you up to speed—"

"That won't be necessary, Jessica," Marita's father said. "If you know Charlotte's history, you are aware that she and her mother lived with my wife and me from the time she was born until Marita purchased a home of her own ten years ago, a time during which Mr. Alessio was almost completely absent from his daughter's life."

And his little blonde wife was still in elementary school. Marita bit the inside of her cheek to keep from speaking out loud.

"I've had Charli every other weekend since she was six years old," Jim said. "And she's known Angel since she was nine."

"Would that be since Charlotte was nine or since Mrs. Alessio was nine?" Marita's father shrugged and looked at the mediator. "Forgive me. I find the age difference confusing."

Angel blushed, but Jim scowled. "Since Charlotte, er, *Charli*, was nine, of course."

Marita grinned. It wasn't like her father to make snarky remarks. Maybe he was afraid that if he didn't, she would, but he had to know that she wouldn't be stupid enough to do anything that would jeopardize her custody of Charli. Still, it was fun watch her father tip Jim off-balance.

"Unfortunately, Judge Mercer," Jessica was saying, "no formal custody agreement has been in place, which is what brought Charlotte's parents here."

Marita's grin vanished.

"Since it appears that both parties are able to offer love and sustenance to Charlotte, there is no reason to deny either parent custody. Therefore, my recommendation is physical custody to both parents, with Charlotte spending two weeks each month with each parent. Most families find it easiest to do Friday to Friday custody with alternating weekends, but if you need help determining a schedule—"

Marita could no longer hear the mediator. A roaring sound had filled her ears, and the room seemed to be spinning.

"Unacceptable," her father was saying, "...had nothing to do with her...no kind of parent...not fair to Charlotte..."

For the second time that morning, Marita wanted to jump out of her seat, grab Charli and run, but she didn't seem to be able to move. Then, suddenly, she realized that her right arm was shaking. She looked down and saw her father's hand on her sleeve, and realized he was shaking her.

"Marita!" her father whispered. "Are you all right?"

"You're white as a sheet," Angel said, speaking for the first time since they'd entered the room. "Jim, get her some water."

"No," Marita said loudly. "I just want Charli."

"Of course Charlotte should stay with you this week, particularly since she seems most comfortable with the current situation," the mediator said. "That will give you a chance to explain things to her and help her get used to the idea before we begin to phase in the new schedule."

"How am I supposed to help her get used to an idea that will break her heart?" Marita knew her voice was high-pitched and frantic, and she hoped no one else could tell she felt as crazy as she sounded.

Jim shook his head, practically rolling his eyes. "What would this phasing in look like?"

But Marita wasn't listening. Jim was going to get away with it. He and his little blonde teenager were going to take her daughter away from her.

She turned to her father. "Is this binding?"

"No," he said crisply. "And I have no intention of allowing it to be." He stood and extended his hand to the mediator. "Thank you for your time, Jessica."

Trembling, Marita stood to follow her father out of the room.

"The mediator said Charli can live with us two weeks each month!" Angel cried. "You can't just do whatever you want!"

Marita's father stopped in the doorway. He raised his eyebrows at Angel then turned to smile at Jessica. "I'm sure you understand why we feel the need to pursue this matter further."

Jim glared at Marita. Though his arm was wrapped protectively around Angel, anger blazed in his eyes, and he looked as though he wanted to clap his free hand over his wife's mouth. "Angel's right," he said. "You can't simply disregard the mediator's findings."

"My opinion isn't binding," Jessica said. "And you have no legal agreement in place. You're both free to continue as you have been."

"What if we don't want to do that?" Angel asked.

"I can meet with you again to see if we can all come to an agreement," Jessica said. "We can also set up a meeting to determine a phase-in plan that will work for everyone. Or, if you wish, you can pursue this further through the courts."

"We're through here," Marita said, moving toward the door.

"You can't just run away and pretend nothing's changed," Jim called after her.

Marita turned on her heel. "Why not? That's what you did when Charli was born."

"I was nineteen years old, Marita, and a sophomore in college. In case you haven't noticed, a lot has changed since then."

"I was sixteen, Jim, but I still figured out how to be a mother."

"Oh, come on, Marita," Jim said. "We both know your parents raised Charli. You weren't any more of a parent during her early childhood than I was."

"At least I was there —"

"And I'm trying to be there now," Jim said. "But you won't let me."

"And how about your parents, Jim? Are they ready to acknowledge their grandchild? Or are they still harboring the delusion that I got pregnant all by myself?"

Marita's father took her arm. "We're finished here," he said. "Thank you for your time, Jessica. We'll be in touch."

Marita let her father lead her out of the room, her stomach churning. Only when she reached the hallway did it hit her that Charli might have heard every word that had been said.

But the hallway was empty. Charli and her grandmother were nowhere in sight.

"Where are they?" Marita started down the hall, her panic re-surfacing as quickly as it had subsided.

Her father caught her by the shoulder and pulled her gently toward him. "Calm down and take a deep breath. I suggested that your mother give Charli a nice, long tour of the courthouse."

Marita smiled and felt her shoulders relax. For the second time that morning, her parents' habit of taking over any situation was working to her advantage.

"So, you and Mom had this all planned?"

"I'm surprised you're not angry."

"No, relieved," Marita said. "I was so furious with Jim that I didn't even think about the fact that Charli could be sitting right outside the door this whole time. Did you know things would turn out this way?"

"I had no way of knowing how things would turn out. I knew, however, that there was a good chance that Jim and the young Mrs. Alessio would look good to a mediator."

"Dad, what am I going to do?"

"You're going to fight for custody."

"What if the judge agrees with the mediator?"

"Don't worry about that now. First things first. Let's collect your mother and Charli and have some lunch. I'm sure your daughter will have a multitude of questions."

I just wish I had better answers.

CHAPTER THREE

"Angel, you have *got* to learn to control your emotions," Jim scolded the moment they were alone on the elevator.

"I'm sorry, honey, but I just couldn't stand it! Why does Marita think she doesn't have to follow the rules?"

Jim pushed the button for the ground floor. "They aren't rules, Angel. At least not yet. The mediator can only make recommendations."

"Well, I don't see what was wrong with the recommendations she made."

Jim looked at her, amused. "You didn't really think Marita would just accept this, did you?"

"Why did we go through this if no one was even going to listen?"

Jim shook his head. "I love that you're so naïve. We're laying groundwork, sweetheart. If the mediator thinks alternating custody is a good arrangement, then there's a good chance a judge will, too."

"I don't know, Jim. I love Charli, but she's never stayed with us for more than a weekend. Consulting with a mediator was one thing, but why fight for custody now when we're trying to start a family of our own?"

"Do you really want Charli to grow up like her mother? She's twelve years old. If we don't get her now, she'll spend the rest of her teenage years with Marita."

"You make it sound like you want to take Charli away from Marita completely!"

The elevator chimed, but neither of them moved. "Would that be such a bad idea?"

Angel's eyes filled with tears. She couldn't imagine anything more cruel than depriving a mother of her child. In fact, it was the only thing she could imagine that was worse than never having a child of her own.

* * * * *

An hour later, Angel sat in the parking lot of Holy Redeemer Community Church, powdering her nose, freshening her lipstick, and wishing it was as easy to freshen her attitude. The mediation had been bad enough, but the thought of Jim actually trying to take Charli away from Marita made her sick to her stomach. She'd believed him when he told her he wanted more time with Charli and more influence over her life. But now, listening to him talk about laying groundwork, Angel was just beginning to grasp how ugly this could get.

Lisa is a transplanted Jersey Girl who has lived in Pennsylvania most of her adult life. After 27 years as an elementary school counselor, Lisa decided to plan her work life around her family life. Now, she works as a writer, adjunct professor, and community education instructor. Lisa is the author of two books inspired by her students, *Acting Assertively* and *Diverse Divorce*. She is also the author of a novel, *Casting the First Stone*, as well as many blogs and articles.

The Punk Test
Cynthia Reeves

Here are some general guidelines for this test.

- Use only a sharpened # 2 pencil. Using any other number pencil will result in a null score.
- Fill in all ovals completely, but do not allow pencil marks to stray outside the ovals. Partial fill-ins will not be counted as answers. Likewise, allowing a mark to stray outside the lines, or to touch another lettered oval, may cause the scanner to read your mark improperly.
- Be sure to erase mistakes thoroughly. The scanner may read shadows as answers and invalidate other answers that may be correct.
- Keep in mind that there is one and only one correct answer to each question.

Let's begin.

Read the following passage carefully and then answer the questions following it based on what is stated or implied.

How to Be a Punk

According to *Webster's Dictionary*, the word "punk" originated in 1596 with the meaning "prostitute." That connotation has been lost in the modern idiom; in fact, quite contrary to the idea of selling oneself for personal benefit, a contemporary punk might be a fierce individualist with nothing to gain by asserting punk status. On the other hand, some embrace punk just because they think it's cool. These punks are in fact the anti-punks, the ones who fail the basic punk test. Punk is a mindset. One shouldn't have to dress or act in any particular way to be punk. Punk means never apologizing to anyone for anything.

1. According to the passage, punk is:
   A. a movement characterized by the adoption of an aggressively unconventional style and the defiance of social norms of behavior
   B. any prepared substance that can be used to cause an incendiary reaction
   C. someone worthless or unimportant
   D. a test of an entirely different nature than this one, in which a moderately sharp object such as a fingernail is scraped over the tenderest flesh of the inner forearm either until blood is drawn or the victim cries out
2. Did you cry out?
3. Excuse me? Yes, it's a simple yes-or-no question. Yes, that question

counted. And no, we can't go back. Tests are all about going on to the next page. Are you ready for the next page?

4. How long does it take to create a 12-inch-long gouge approximately ¼-inch deep and ¼-inch wide using only the edge of a fingernail?

    A. 10 minutes

    B. 30 minutes

    C. Until the tormentor draws blood

    D. Until the victim cries out

I'm sorry. "Sixty minutes" is not a valid answer. I admit, it's a difficult question, not your run-of-the-mill mathematics. Please don't get upset. Studies have shown that anxiety causes test performance to suffer unnecessarily.

How about we move on to the essay? The essay gives you an opportunity to demonstrate how effectively you express ideas. To obtain the best results, you should take several minutes to brainstorm before you begin. Here's the question:

5. Henry James wrote: "One is oneself a fine consequence." Discuss this quotation in light of the most significant events of your life.

You have 25 minutes. Begin.

   ***

Time's up.

Why is your sheet blank? Were the directions unclear? If you don't write anything, I can't give you any credit. There, there, perhaps you can make the points up on the next question.

6. Why did you let him do it?

7. Why are you crying?

Okay, this was a stupid idea. Let's just throw away the test and talk. Tests are subjective anyway, even the most seemingly objective tests. Don't they all, every one, depend upon your point of reference? So when we ... oh, wait a second, not literally we, since I'm alone, since I've long since lost touch with you ...

   ***

Let's start over.

8. When we (forgive me) say punk now—now being 2011, 42 years after the fact of our ten-year-old girls' lives—when we say punk, what do we mean? Someone humiliating someone else for the sake of a laugh?

9. Is humiliation as painful as the pain of having your arm gouged by a boy who only wants to hear you cry?

10. I admit it, Jane, that last question was unfair. A leading question. Let's cut to the chase, as they say. Fourth grade. It was fourth grade, wasn't it? Sister Thomas Michael Joseph. The nun who walked up and down the

aisles snapping a ruler against her open palm? Slap, slap, slap. Do you recall the way we lined up that day, boys on one side of the classroom, girls on the other, both sides wearing uniformly white, long-sleeved shirts that our mothers had starched that morning? Too scared of Sister Thomas Michael Joseph to assume any kind of attitude other than abject terror?

11. Worlds away, young boys were fighting and dying, young boys not much older than the boys on the other side of the classroom. Do you recall that offensive? It was all over the news. Tet, it was called. Wipe out South Vietnam, and by extension America, all that we knew, in one *incendiary reaction.* That was the Viet Cong plan. Were they punks? What did we know? Our world was that classroom and Sister Thomas Michael Joseph and seventy-five of us lined up one day in two perfect rows, the toes of our shoes touching the same dark seam in the white-flecked, gray linoleum. Remember that day, Jane?

12. Here are two tangents:

    A. That day, sun streamed through the classroom's wall of plate-glass windows.

    B. Three years later, a boy named Dean threw a desk through those same windows. He was taken away, and I never saw him again either.

You're right. These aren't questions. The details aren't relevant to the story, may not even be true. But they do add a sense of place and time, don't you think? What writers call "setting," which is so valuable to the best stories. But I'd argue that this sort of digression is different than telling a story that doesn't address the question. There are always questions. Which leads me to this:

13. Perhaps recollection is a simple mathematical equation. Something like: Memory equals distance multiplied by time. How long *does* it take, Jane, to be scarred for life?

14. That was a trick question, but this isn't: How long did it take Sister Thomas Michael Joseph to reach you, Jane?

15. Unbutton your cuff, Sister says to each of us in turn. Unroll your sleeve. Standing there, I wonder, Did I scrub the line of dirt from the crease of my elbow this morning? I wonder, What will Mom think when I flunk Cleanliness? A boy named Ricky is led away by Father McCabe, who's covering Ricky's forearm with his left hand. Why? We find out soon enough. This strange drill is only a new form of erasure, like kneeling in the dark before the priest, like trying to stop the pounding of one's heart while waiting for the confessional screen to slide open, waiting to say, *Bless me, Father, for I have sinned.*

16. I'm right behind you, Jane. It's your turn. The crust of the scab swells to a fingernail's width as your sleeve folds into itself. Higher and higher, past the crease of your elbow where there is a thin ridge of dirt. But Sister is not concerned with Cleanliness today. She's focused on Godliness. When the scab finally tapers into the flesh of your pale, thin bicep, I think, How long, Jane? But I say nothing. Father McCabe takes you away, too. Then they tell us this fad, this *punk test*, is a mortal sin, a violation of the body. Didn't they call women by men's names? Didn't they know all about self-abnegation?

17. Sometimes late at night, lying in the dark and angry dark, I imagine what your scar must look like now. If there is a now. *Are* you listening, Jane? I imagine the dark and angry mark. Was yours a stray line touching every one of us, and one we, like scanners endlessly scanning lettered ovals, read improperly?

18. Was the punk test like entering someone with intent to love, but also to harm?

19. And who was that boy who violated you? Did Sister Thomas Michael Joseph or Father McCabe even think to ask? We both know the answer to that question.

20. Let me be honest with myself for once. Can anybody rescue anybody? There are only two possible answers:

    A. You can't.
    B. You don't.

Cynthia Reeves's novella *Badlands* (MU Press 2008) was awarded Miami University Press's Novella Prize. Her fiction, essays, and poetry have appeared in *Colorado Review*, *Crab Orchard Review*, *Waxwing*, *Booth* and elsewhere. Reeves has won numerous awards and honors, including several Pushcart Prize nominations and prizes in Columbia's Fiction Contest, the DeMott Short Prose Contest (Quarter After Eight), New Millennium's Short Short Fiction Contest, and Potomac Review's Fiction Contest. A graduate of Warren Wilson College's MFA program, Reeves currently teaches in Bryn Mawr College's Creative Writing Program and Rosemont College's MFA Program. She has been a visiting writer at Miami University and Penn State, conducted classes on the novella and experimental prose forms at conferences and seminars nationwide, and taught creative non-fiction in the Philadelphia Young Writers Program.

A Gala Occasion
Dorothy Ryan

Like two apples
left behind on the tree
we are no longer
lush juicy sweet
golden delicious.
Past our prime,
we are more
maturing winesap.
In bed, we joke
about my arthritic foot,
his bionic knee.
Hopefully,
the knee won't buckle
my foot won't cramp.
We turn to embrace
and slowly, steadily, ripen.

Dorothy Ryan's poems have been published in *America*, (she was a finalist Foley Prize), *The Christian Science Monitor*, *Naugatuck River Review*, *Paterson Literary Review*, *The Pedestal*, *Rambunctious Review*, and *Stillwater Review*, among others. She has published online and in national and regional newspapers. She has work in *Paterson: The Poet's City* (The Poetry Center, PCCC, 2005), *To Love One Another: Poems Celebrating Marriage* (Grayson Books, 2002) and *Love Over 60* (Mayapple Press, 2010). Her chapbook, *Animal Weaver*, was published in 2002 (Carpenter Press). Born in New York, she lives in New Jersey with her husband of 45 years and their adult daughter with autism. She volunteers at a local library, where she is "Library Poet." She is working on a book of poems.

Rest Cure
Frances Boyle

- i -

Here's Jack, lanky in a cut-down suit, narrow-chested but chippy as life in the rattle scrape east end of Montreal can make an English-speaking kid. He's got Catholicism in common with the French kids, but they want to know "es-tu canadien or es-tu anglais?" They push; he pushes back.

He doesn't go looking for a fight, though, not like Ger. A year and a half older, Gerry is shorter than Jack but solid and scrappy. Real tough. Tough enough to take down a big guy older than him, boys and men crowding round to watch him fight. Even the guy's father, hands by his sides, face like an old sock, a crumpled handkerchief. Jack asks, "why don't you stop it?" The man shrugs, real tired looking, says it's a lesson. Next time the son'll watch who he picks on.

Katie and Helen are working. They have good jobs at the hospital, doing research for a doctor, mixing things in labs, making people well. The doctor made a big impression on his sisters, talking about people dying, and not enough beds for them all. The charity wards are full, and the rest cure is the only thing for the consumption. Worried about his cough, the girls pulled strings for him. That's how Jack ended up in this place, like a bump on a log. The doctors call it chasing the cure, but Jack knows that's a load of bull, you can't chase anything when you're lying still.

Blue bowl, often white-streaked, often grey. You don't see skies like that in the city, and his mother and the girls are agog over the beauty when they come to see him. They make the same winding train trip Jack had taken, steam whistle wailing out, sounding lonely as hell and that's how he feels in this bed, this basket on wheels. He has to lie there all the time, on this porch and in the dark night dormitories full of the snores and farts of strangers, old men and young ones, many no older than Jack.

The blue bowl is inverted, held up by the mountains. On the porch, lying there, all in a row, Jack feels the air cold and oh-so-good-for-you fresh. Out with the bad air, in with the good. But if he's got to chase a cure, he'd rather be chasing it the way the kids on the block used to chase each other, or the precious puck the French kids stole from them, leaving them with nothing but horse turds to play shinny with, Jack and Ger and the guys on Rachel Street.

Some of the people are really sick, skeleton skinny, coughing themselves hollow. Jack measures the distance down the slope toward the lake when one of them starts coughing. Others are like Jack, here because ... Jack is hard-pressed to say exactly why he's here but there was whispered talk in the pantry over dinner dishes. Ma and sisters that worried about him. The consumption is in the family. Aunt Claire died of it five years ago. Whispering over weak-chested, tall and gangly Jack, wrists out of the suits Ma made by cutting down their father's old police uniforms. He left a couple of uniforms when he died, the last Ma will have to work with.

How could they send me away? he wonders; I was just starting to make money at the factory, dammit. Man's money, almost. Not like the message-boy money they were so proud to hand over to Ma when he and Ger worked at the Birks building.

They'd sit in that narrow dusty room with its wood floors that creaked, itching for the bell to ring, to spring them, he and Gerry each waiting a turn to carry something, a message or a parcel, it didn't matter. To be out running, just flying, through the building, down the alleyways. Ger would beat him to the bell, especially when the message had to go far. They'd wind up wrestling and rolling around on the floor. Jack got the worst of it, Ger was that tough. Beat Jack up bad one time. Ma wanted to know what happened to his face, so Jack told her the French kids did it. Katie didn't like them fighting, not at all. She was the one who got them the jobs, in the building where she typed all day.

Now she and Helen were working for that doctor. That's how he got here, the girls put in a word. Ma told him how lucky he was. Lots of people with the consumption, dying of it like her sister, and never enough beds. Less than a hundred here, and a smaller place on the other slope for the Jews, that's what Albert tells Jack when they first get talking.

Albert used to be a patient. He caught the cure, but he'll never be well enough to go back to the foundry. They let him work here. He does odd jobs, pushes the meal cart. He wheels beds out onto the porch every morning and every afternoon for the patients to take the air, wheels them back to the long sleeping rooms.

This is no place for me, Jack thinks. It's fine for the rich snots to lie there reading their newspapers and fat books. They're used to sitting around, some flunky bringing them their breakfasts. No big deal to have metal bowls brought in so they can wash and shave. Not Jack. He started shaving last year. He'd break the ice on the bucket, the way their grown brothers had, when he and Ger were whippersnappers watching them. No one ever brought him a bowl.

It's cold on the porch sometimes, other times hot. Buzzing hot, but all Jack keeps is cold. He feels it in his young bones, feels the days line up like boxcars on a siding: waiting to be wheeled outside, waiting to be moved indoors. Nothing ever new except when the doctor walks through, his coat snapping behind him. And visiting days, his sisters going on about people in the parish, Ma sighing over how the mountains remind her of being a girl in Ste. Sophie. It's always the same slow rhythm. At what point does blue streaked with white become white streaked with blue, a milky bowl?

Once in a while, they bring a different bowl and he has to spit. There's no blood, never. Albert will say that Jack had none of those germs, the ones that make the consumption, but much later when he helps Jack pack his grip.

Albert jokes with Jack. He calls him the sleepwalker. Pretends Jack's last name is Dempsey. He's talking about those first few nights when Jack would get out of bed. He wasn't doing anything bad – just got up to peer through windows, see what his feet looked like in the moonlight, find out what was beyond that door. It took two orderlies to strap him down, he fought the ties so. Albert puts down the putty knife he's using for the storm windows, throws his arms and head around, laughing. His hands are open fists. The big orderly, Charlie, finally landed one good punch, Albert says, and Jack didn't give them any more trouble. Now he settles down peaceful as a babe every night.

It's long ago to Jack, but the nurses still pin him with their sharp gazes. Not that there's anything he could do in the white shift they traded for his suit, nowhere he could go. Snow sprawls on the mountains beyond. Sometimes the hillsides are green, sometimes parched like a faded yellow blanket, but always they slope away, out of reach.

He thinks about his family. Ma off to Westmount every day, to do for Mrs. Marler. She brings home Mrs. Marler's old clothes, still perfectly good, for the girls. Brings home Mrs. Marler ways: doilies on the arms of the sofa, and *pass the peas please*. His father would slam his fist on the table so the dishes rattled, mouth pursed, his voice shrill: "Mrs. Marler, Mrs. Jesus Marler, for crissake!" But the old man is gone. The pleurisy took him in less than a month, leaving just two sets of uniforms for Ma to make over.

The girls are smart in Mrs. Marler's made-over clothes. Katie and Helen have good paying jobs. All the girls play piano, like Ma. They have manners like Mrs. Marler's daughters.

The older brothers are grown and gone to the lumber camp or the merchant navy. Gerry never comes to visit Jack. Scared of the germs, Helen says. He wants to come but he can't, Katie says. He's apprenticing with a tile-setter. He's home only for bed, and for the meat and cold potatoes Ma puts aside on the hob. Time off for Mass, of course.

It doesn't sound much like Gerry to Jack. He can't imagine Ger working hard, toeing the line. But everyone has to pull their weight now the old man's gone.

So, why send Jack away when he'd started to make real money? On the delivery run, he'd race up and down stairs with boxes full of stockings in their paper packets, so quick that Ernie hardly had time to finish his smoke. He taught himself to drive by watching Ernie's feet work the clutch, the brake, the gas. Ernie sometimes let him drive back after the last deliveries. And the factory paid better. Those three months when he had a fatter pay envelope to carry home to Ma, he didn't mind the big room steamy from the vats, his fingers wrinkled and hands cramped from putting wet stockings on the forms.

He thinks about Ger working with the tile-setter, handing him tools, learning how to make the pieces go in straight. He has to make himself not think about Ger. He looks at the slice of lake he can see from the porch, counts the trees that block his view, looks at the sky. There's always the sky, even when it's years he has to count.

It's nearly spring again when Jack finally puts his suit back on, feels fabric strain over his chest when he does the buttons up. He rides the train back to the city alone, just like when he came. He never once tested positive, practically a year, that's what Albert tells him as he leaves.

- ii -

The factory's not taking on any more men. Jobs in the city are harder to find. Jack takes ones far away. He goes to the Gaspé, then up north in Ontario.

The north is snow crunch and fly buzz: Deep River, Chapleau. Each town another tie on tracks that go on and on, rumble and hum. Every place the same cold stretch of distance, whether there's white or green beneath the blue bowl.

He doesn't see the family often. He paces the wooden floors of rented rooms in railway towns, relearns silence in gold-brown liquid at the bottom of a glass and the gentle burn that starts in his stomach. He drinks in his room, or in bars, at tables a little away from the lumberjacks who sing and swear and down glasses, though not with the railwayman.

Montreal, when he goes back for visits, is noisy bustle. Hugs from Ma and sisters, little nephews and nieces, slaps on the back and nights in the tavern with Ger. He pulls Gerry out of fights, or backs him up. When they put on uniforms, they make a fine pair: the tall one and the short one, Air Force and Army. Both broad-shouldered now, and sharp. They turn a head or two.

Then a different trip. Back, for Ma's funeral. Telegraph poles tick by and the train jostles. The rumble of the tracks builds. There's pressure in his ears and behind his eyes. Tightness rises from his chest to his throat, squeezes, chokes him. A swig or two from his flask helps, but he doesn't drink more. He won't shame the family at the funeral.

But afterwards, his brothers-in-law gone after only one round, Jack roars through taverns. With Ger shipped out to England, it's not like it was. He just drinks until he stumbles back, waking his sister's house, roars some more, drops and sleeps.

The next morning, there's little Maureen showing her brother the hole Uncle Jack punched in the wall. His head is muzzy, and he's anxious to be on his way, furlough over. He carries the train's rattle with him to where his unit is stationed.

The buzz stays in his head long after the C.O. comes to the barracks with the news. Gerry, killed overseas. Didn't even see action, poor bugger. An enlisted man pulled a knife on him, in a barroom fight.

Jack never makes it home again. He knows other cities, lives in one with a view of mountains that make the Laurentians seem like hills. He meets someone at the office where he's taken a job. She's a woman from Toronto, but Catholic, and he accompanies her to Mass. She agrees to marry him though they think they're probably too old to start a family. To their surprise, a baby girl, arrives after they've moved to another new city.

He puts down the bottle because his wife says he must. He gets dry and stays dry. There are groups she wants him to go to. He tries them, but it's all talk. So he goes it alone, never takes another drink.

They have another daughter. Their last move is to the prairie, where the bowl is wide, no hills to be seen.

- iii -

The blinds half-lowered, the blue or milky blue or grey outside is shut out to allow him and the others a discreet snooze, all in their chairs. They're all old, and mostly women. The people here don't strap him down. They did in the hospital when it hurt so bad to cough and his chest was full – pneumonia, they said. He kept wanting to sit up and catch a breath. But he didn't fight the ties, just worked and worried at them until he came here.

What he is doing in this place, so still and quiet? He has a department to run, a family to see to, man's responsibilities that he shoulders gladly. His children visit, with pictures of their mother. *Bitter* is the word he finds as he realizes he remembers nothing about her. They remind him again, but gently, that she died last year.

The girls are doing well. He's proud of them, their good jobs. It was their doing, he remembers now. They brought him. A fine daughter on either side for the long ride – he glowed with pride. But why the hell must he stay, with these old women, staring at flickering colours on a screen?

It's still now. Jack hears the women's voices, the quiet clatter of cutlery – at a distance. The years slope away. He is part of those hills.

Frances Boyle is a poet and fiction writer. She is the author of *Light-carved Passages* (BuschekBooks, 2014) and the chapbook *Portal Stones*. She won Tree Press's chapbook contest, the Diana Brebner Prize, and first place in *This Magazine's* Great Canadian Literary Hunt for poetry. Her poetry and short stories have appeared in Canadian and American literary magazines, and anthologies on subjects from Hitchcock to form poetry to mother/daughter relationships. Featured at Ottawa's Tree Reading Series as a "Hot Ottawa Voice," Frances serves on the editorial board of *Arc Poetry Magazine*. Originally from the Canadian prairie, Frances now lives in Ottawa, the nation's capital.

Grove of the Patriarchs
Grace Marcus

I am the first child my mother never wanted.

That I have two brothers and a sister is a testament to her docility, not her change of heart. My earliest memory is of her perfume, an exotic, spicy scent, and of her dark hair swinging down around her pale and pretty face when she rescued the hem of her dress from my grasp. I was always reaching out for her. This is not selective memory. In photos she is ever lovely, and I am ever longing—one chubby arm outstretched—to touch her. One day (I must have been five or six years old and whining for her attention) she told me, "I'm not your mother." And, for a moment, I believed her. It's when I noticed for the first time my mother's dreamy blindness and deafness, inhabiting what world I didn't know. All I knew was that she was unhappy when summoned back to mine.

For all his faults, my father was the one who took care of us when we were sick, staying with us until we fell asleep. "*Frère Jacques, Frère Jacques. Dormez-vous? Dormez-vous?*" he'd chant over and over but I'd resist, waiting once more for the '*Sonnez les matines. Sonnez les matines,*' loving the sweet cadence of his voice, his hand on my forehead.

Since he walked out on her, it falls to me to be my mother's caretaker, not that she needs one yet. But if it comes down to that, it will be me. My brothers live on the east coast and my sister Sharon, who lives in Vancouver—Washington, not Canada—and close enough to drive down in a few hours, hasn't spoken to our mother in years. "You're a sap, Suzanne," she tells me. "You can't change the past."

I've taken today off from my job at the *Puget Sound Views* (it's a monthly magazine and we just put the January issue to bed) to drive my mother to a cardiologist in Seattle for a consult about a condition that causes her heart to slow and lurch disconcertingly. She and I live on opposite sides of the Narrows Bridge, I'm in Tacoma and she's in Gig Harbor. I leave early enough to first drive down to Point Defiance Park to walk the waterfront, a salve for the resentment I will inevitably feel when she fails to evidence any interest in those parts of my world that do not intersect with hers.

A mile long crescent of walkway snakes from the parking lot at the boat launch to the beach along Commencement Bay in the penumbra of the Cascades. Mount Rainier wears a corona of clouds, so I can't see its distinctive ram's head shape, even though the weather is unusually fine for December. That's where I planned to be today for my ritual respite after the jumpy rush of making the deadline—up in Mount Rainier National Park on a small island in the middle of the Ohanapecosh River, at the Grove of the Patriarchs, filling my lungs with oxygen from the ancient trees. That stand of Douglas fir, western hemlock, and red cedar has been growing undisturbed for nearly 1,000 years, the river protecting the Grove from fire, the gods protecting it from all else. I am fascinated by the elegant symbiosis of the nurse logs, which perpetuate that lush forest. The fallen trees decay by degrees into a carpet of mosses. Then lichens, mushrooms and fern transform them into nurseries for cedar and conifer seedlings. There are nurse logs here at Point Defiance as well, along Five Mile Drive, but I've run out of morning.

There's no bridge traffic at this hour so I can easily hazard glimpses down at the choppy swells and the blue-gray ropes of rip tides in the Narrows. On the other side of the bridge, I take the second exit and drive around the harbor where the marinas are filled with masts soldiering in the breeze, before looping onto the access road to my mother's house. I turn left at the crooked Madrona tree, drive down the unpaved lane and park on the gravel. Her house, rented since my parents' divorce three years ago, is shoebox plain, with dated appliances, and drab carpeting but is situated on a sandy spit of beachfront amid grander homes. Inside it smells pleasantly of bracken from the stones and shells and driftwood she has placed on every windowsill, in every shallow bowl, her only contribution to this furnished house. Her decorative stamp is outdoors, in the whimsical sculptures, the tiles embedded in the pathways, a hot tub enclosed by a filmy forest of pampas grass.

My mother beams her hello from the open doorway. Nothing personal. It's the same smile she offers everyone. She used to be beautiful, with a hint of animal wildness peeking out in the otherwise buttoned-up old photos, her belt tied askew at her cinched waist, a bit of tooth bared between the dark lips, her hip cocked and knees aslant, as provocative as she dared, it seemed to me.

Even now at nearly seventy, she is prettier than I, with her thick hair—streaked and cropped spiky-short—and espresso eyes, lips that redden as if dipped in persimmons, even without lipstick. She wears an ivory silk blouse with a narrow black skirt and a light wool jacket the color of plums. Two-inch heels and tinted stockings show off her elegant ankles and calves. I am raggedy with lack of sleep and rumpled for lack of clean laundry.

Both my daughters were home over Thanksgiving break—Elise from Boston, where she lives with her father during the school year, and Kit from Ann Arbor, where she lives with her lover, also named Kit, also a woman. When the girls are home, except for work, I put the rest of my life on hold. Not out of obligation or sacrifice but because I enjoy their company; Elise's mordant wit and discerning intellect; Kit's dead-on mimicry, her hilarious political rants. I'd like them even if they weren't my daughters.

We cook together and scout thrift stores, ride the ferries and walk the waterfront. Sail in good weather. They catch up with their friends and each other when they're home. But they've stopped visiting their grandparents. My father berates my former husband to Elise, who adores him, and crudely mocks Kit's relationship. "You just haven't met the right guy, honey," he told her. "Believe me, he'd change your tune."

My mother, on the other hand, pretends that neither the girls' father nor Kit's lover exist.

"I had a bad night," my mother tells me, offering her cheek to be kissed.

"You look wonderful." I say this as if it were an accusation.

"Oh, well . . ." she waves her hand, dismissive. "I felt it though." She rests her fingertips in a cage over her heart.

"What? What did you feel?" I always have to shape her language to understand her, she's maddeningly vague.

"My heart," she says.

"Felt it what, Mom? Stop? Slow? Hesitate?"

"Just different, you know. Like it's been."

My mother has unwittingly chosen my profession. I untangle syntax, un-mix metaphors; interrogate reporters until I know the story as well as they, so their articles will read with clarity and grace. I sigh. It doesn't matter what she says, anyway. We will have empirical evidence soon. The exam, EKG, the labs.

My mother waits until I pull onto I-5 and am dodging traffic before she tells me she has been seeing my father. The way she says it, I know it isn't for coffee.

"He's married," I say, although that's not what worries me.

"Maybe it's better this way."

"Why? So he can beat her up and date you?"

"Don't be melodramatic, Suzanne." Her tone is mild. "Your father never struck me."

When I feel compassionate, I remind myself that she was constricted in every possible way: by poverty and gender, education and class. What she had in abundance was imagination. It was how, I understood later, she could pretend my father was exhausted or worried when he was overbearing or cruel. How she could reframe his badgering as concern, his insults as instructive. The dreamy quality that kept her at a remove from me, from us, was how she survived. The pity was she couldn't imagine herself free.

The cardiologist is bald except for a low-lying fringe of woolly grey hair, is extremely tall. Tall, and good-looking in a coarse, sensual way. His fingers are thick, his mouth wide. He swivels in his chair and rests one ankle on the opposite knee, his thigh a long and solid plank, his shoe like a small boat.

"I haven't seen you before, Mrs. . ." he glances down at her chart, ". . . Garner, have I?"

"It's Ms.," my mother says. "And yes, I had a consult in August."

He puts down the chart and studies her. "I think I would have remembered you." He manages to make this sound provocative.

He stands and extends his hand, "Come, let me listen before we do the EKG."

He helps her onto the examination table, tells her to unbutton her blouse. She is, I see, wearing a lacy camisole. He slips the stethoscope under its frothy trim. Her breast disappears under his cupped hand.

"Fifty beats per minute," the doctor says. "Any dizziness? Nausea?"

"Sometimes."

"Which?" he asks her. "How often?"

Good luck, I think, trying to understand my mother.

He takes her hand and tries again. "How about now? Do you feel light-headed now?"

It infuriates me that this man is flirting with my mother—and not in a patronizing way—some remnant of her glory days clings to her, some superannuated estrogen patch or pheromone. My boyfriends, my husband, all of them were taken with her. I don't know how my father stood it. No, that's a lie.

My father is the sort of man who likes his women beautiful. Beautiful and frail. He does, of course, resent them for it later.

"Christ, Adele, must I do every little goddamned thing for you?" he would say after my mother handed him a light bulb or a recalcitrant pickle jar.

"Of course you must, Mitchell," she'd say, and laugh as she rubbed up against him, the sensuous gesture revolting to my teenage self. Was it that or the way in which my father was captivated?

He always got the best parts of her. And when my father was away, at work or on a business trip, it was as though she went away as well. From the time I was twelve, I became the woman of the house in his absence, signing permission slips, helping with homework, defrosting the ground beef for dinner. My mother wore aprons fussily, like a wardrobe in a play. Pots got burned and dinners ruined amid chapters of a book.

I am fulminating about all this when my mother blinks three times then slumps to the floor.

The doctor kneels beside her, bends his ear to her mouth. When he places his hands between her breasts, it takes me a second to realize it's CPR. "Get my nurse," he tells me. "Now. Move!"

I intercept the nurse in the hallway. "My mother collapsed . . . he wants you . . ."

The placid-faced Filipina races past me into a room, then pops right back out, like in a cartoon, dragging a red metal cart behind her. She summons another nurse who rushes into the same room and wheels out a gurney.

It's only minutes before the doctor is running alongside the gurney, two nurses in attendance, the Filipina straddled across my mother's chest, her hands like pistons revving up my mother's heart. I run behind until they disappear into the service elevator at the end the corridor. I'm punching the elevator buttons when the receptionist tells me they've taken my mother to the Cardiac Care Unit.

"Fifth floor," she tells me. "Bear right."

I call Sharon from the family waiting room. "I'll come down," she says.

I know she means for me, not our mother. The kindness undoes me. "Okay," I manage through the knot in my throat. "Good," I whisper.

"Suze?"

I can't speak.

"Suzanne. You've done your best, damn it."

"Her, too," I say, and hang up before Sharon can tell me that's bullshit.

While I wait, I close my eyes and conjure the hushed embrace of the Grove of the Patriarchs, immerse myself in its green glory until I am as tranquil and still as the trees themselves, and so I can't believe it when the handsome doctor comes out with that look on his face, the one that says everything isn't okay and never will be again.

The room has a ghoulish green glow, all fluorescence and scrubs and easily washed plastic chairs. Everything else is white, the crib-like hospital beds, the linens, the bathroom fixtures exposed to passers-by.

I edge past the patient in the bed closest to the door; my heart knocking in my chest, to look for her but the second bed is empty. I double-check the slip of paper in my hand. Room 3605-A. The first bed. I spin around. I didn't recognize her because this time she has gone so far away that she's never coming back.

I know this even before the doctor arrives and tells me it wasn't her heart, after all, but a burst aneurysm that caused the stroke, which has spared her heart but ravaged her brain.

My breaths seem to enter my chest through a long narrow tube, one cold milliliter at a time. I back out of the room grateful for the obligation I have to call the others. I call my brothers first. They take it in stride. To them our mother has been as impartial and reliable as a nurse log, giving off nutrients but little else once they took off on their own.

"I'm sorry, Suze," they tell me, acknowledging the loss is mine alone.

I call Sharon but get her voice mail. I don't leave a message. I call my father last, reluctant to subject my mother to either his scrutiny or his lack of regard. Until I can make contact with Sharon, I walk the streets, wandering over to Pioneer Square, then into the lobby of the Alexis Hotel where I buy a pack of cigarettes in the gift shop. It's been a decade since I've smoked but I decide I've been prudent for too long, that I should have been bolder and said my piece when I still had the chance. Three cigarettes later, I throw away the pack and dial Sharon again.

She cries when I tell her. Great gulping sobs which astonish me. I'd expected her to comfort me but it's the other way around and when I hang up, I realize that she must have harbored the same secret hope all the years she'd been ridiculing mine.

The hospital room is dark now, except for the frenetic flickering of the TV. The remote is pinned to the sheet near my mother's head, the stagy voices and static-y soundtrack leaking onto her pillow. I can't tell if she's listening but she's not watching the screen, her eyes are closed. *Wait.* If she turned on the TV, then perhaps she's trying to work her way back to speech, back to comprehension.

The nurse's voice startles me. "We turn it on for them. Sometimes it helps," he says as he fastens the blood pressure cuff onto my mother's arm.

"Is it helping now?" I ask, a tendril of hope taking root in my chest.

He shrugs. "Hard to tell."

As soon as he leaves, I stand close to the bed. "Mom," I say. "Mom. It's me."

She looks up at the sound of my voice. Her gaze slides down my face to my hand, which she seizes in a fierce grip.

"Mom," I try again and this time she doesn't even look up, but just tightens her hold on me until my hand aches and her nails inscribe their hieroglyphics in my flesh. One by one, I pry her fingers loose and cradle them between my palms until they slacken.

"It's okay, Mom, I'm right here." I tuck her in and brush the damp hair away from her still lovely face.

I station the green plastic chair where she can see me and settle into its cool, unyielding embrace, prepared to stay until she falls asleep. She reaches for me through the bed-rails. I take her hand and begin, *"Frère Jacques, Frère Jacques. Dormez-vous? Dormez-vous?"*

Grace Marcus is a member of the Women's Fiction Writers Association. Her work has been published in *Philadelphia Stories, The Bucks County Writer Magazine, Adanna Literary Journal, The Writer's Eye,* and *Women on Writing.* Her novel, *Visible Signs,* was a semi-finalist in the William Faulkner Creative Writing Competition. Her short story collaborations with writer A.L. Sirois have been published in *Flash Fiction Online.* Grace holds a Master's in Theatre Arts from Montclair University. Her checkered past includes stints as an actress, waitress, social worker, newspaper editor, and radio and cable TV show producer. Grace, a Brooklyn native, now lives in Bucks County, Pennsylvania.

Facebook Lies
Deborah A. Miller-Collins

Like most evenings, I unwind at my computer—check my email, log onto Facebook and start scrolling. Zip past the Which-Breaking-Bad-Character-Are-You quiz, my cousin's latest anti-Obama rant, and a half dozen George Takei posts.

Then your face pops up.

And stops my heart.

Not your face now, not the fifty-something profile pic I've seen almost daily since the Internet reconnected us. Not the face I've seen enjoying cookouts, waving kids off to college, kissing that first grandchild. Not the seasoned face that writes friendly comments on my posted pics—vacation photos of my hubby and me or of our now-grown boys. It's been a blessing, my old friend.

No, this is a photo of that nineteen-year-old boy, my first love, from so long ago. The boy I thought was gone forever. And, oh God, I didn't know until just now how much I've missed him.

His blue eyes look right into the camera—so intense that it feels like he's looking straight through me. That intensity that melted me so many years ago melts me again. It takes my breath away.

And I realize the girl I was back then, the one I thought was gone forever, is still here, too. After all these years and changes—marriages, kids, career—that fire still burns.

I loved you so.

I let myself sink back into warm feelings of hazy memories. I'd forgotten how young we once were.

Finally, I catch my breath. Unlock my gaze, return to reality.

And see what I had somehow ignored in those first few moments.

You're not alone in the picture. You and a young woman lean your heads together. She smiles at the camera, too. You both wear those new-love smiles. Your comment reads: *I treasure that moment 35 years ago that brought us together. Happy anniversary to the love of my life!*

And now I see this post of yours for what it really is. My breathing catches again, and that fire I felt just a moment ago burns with a different heat, just like it did way back when.

All that intensity—it was for her. The girl you started seeing while you and I were still a couple. The girl you dumped me for.

It's not like I haven't seen pictures of her before. I've seen dozens—of her, of you, your family, your vacations—pictures of your life now, of your grown-up life. Just as you've seen me with the love of my grown-up life.

But this picture.

It's an artifact, really, of that time in my life when you tore my heart out. I haven't seen that young man in ages; I tore up every picture I had of him when I found out. Every photo, every letter.

The two of you there, sitting on the concrete steps of your parents' cottage at Myrtle Beach—you met her there, didn't you? The sun shines, and the day looks warm, though a breeze stirs your hair and hers. You look so happy together. That buttercup she holds, you gave it to her, didn't you? Did you touch it to her chin first and then kiss her? Did you think of me at all that day? Did she know about me? Did you have anguished talks after a night of love-making about how to deal with me now that the two of you found real love? Did she love you more because it hurt you so much to hurt me?

Did you think about me at all when you posted this, you fucker?

Below the photo, Facebook informs the world that fifty-four people "Like" this photo. Fifty-four people like seeing you two together. The knot in my gut tightens just a bit more.

Sigh.

I click the mouse.

Now it's fifty-five.

Congrats, you guys, I write. *35 years! Wishing you many more!*

Deborah Miller-Collins lives and writes in upstate New York with her husband and two teenage daughters. She has been teaching high school English for 20-something years.

An Ordinary Housewife
Laura Bobrow

From the grandeur of his lofty palace throne
the king has said my name and dubbed me knight.
And of that stuff my vivid dreams are made
till daylight comes. I find myself alone,

a pillow-tousled wench whose visions might
remain one moment more before they fade.
Dare I go slay a dragon? I'm afraid.
My quest's to have my pancakes turn out right.

I would not have the skill, I must confess,
to rescue a fair maiden from her plight.
I trudge out to the kitchen, just a crone
in slippers and a robe, not silken dress.

I wear no helmet. Not of the noblesse,
I bear nobody's standard but my own.

Nationally-acclaimed storyteller Laura J. Bobrow (see www.laurajbobrow.com) offers these poems from the unique perspective of an octogenarian. She is the author of two picture books and three chapbooks. Her work has appeared worldwide in more than 50 venues.

Revlon Shade No. 37
Vickie A. Carr

When Mrs. Krupps died, as usual the men in the family were called to clean up the mess. They found her in the kitchen of what had once been the family ranch, slumped face down, over a small stool by the kitchen sink. She had apparently been preparing to climb up and retrieve the last bottle of liquor in the house from the dim, oily shelves overhead. Later they learned she'd probably been dead for two hours and comatose for ten hours before that, before a neighbor found her and called Mr. Krupps to come and see about things. The oldest boy, Chester, was visiting when the call came, and learned of his mother's death through the unnatural tremor in his father's voice. "Oh no," his father's monotone swerved. "Oh no."

It was difficult for Chester to tell what his father might be thinking as they drove across town that evening. He had not heard that kind of emotion breaking in his father's calm voice in years. It was late fall, and though it was well past the dinner hour, a rind of white-gray light curled around the horizon. Above it the sky was a snarl of timorous, gray clouds threatening to rain that finally splattered in few, huge, random drops onto the windshield as they pulled into the driveway. There was the house in front of them--a long, low ranch built on a slab in the early fifties, and nearly identical to every other house on the street.

Even with the dark gathering in the shrubbery on the front lawn, he could clearly see its color: a bright, apple green. His mother had chosen it a few years back, and then been wild when the dry paint did not match the color in her imagination. *That's not apple-blossom green, it's lime-green. There's a difference. A whole world of difference! We had an apple tree in our backyard when I was a girl and that is absolutely not the color. Why, that's the color of vomit, and I won't live in a house that looks like something you'd spit up into a toilet, she'd said.* She had tried to insist then and there that they repaint the house, but Mr. Krupps refused. And so she'd complained to her children, her neighbors, the hardware dealer who had sold them the paint, and loudest of all to her husband, who was color-blind and penny-wise, and drove off to his job at the plant each morning, leaving her and the house behind. "We'll paint the house again in a few years," he said calmly," and you can choose a whole new color."

It was one of the few times Chester remembered his father flatly standing up to his mother, and now he felt it had probably been for the best. For later, he'd discovered what his father and most of the neighbors had known for years—that his mother was stark-raving mad. As they proceeded up the walk, his father looked grim and serious; his normally erect shoulders sloped forward in his cardigan sweater. He had clear, straight features, a sharp nose, sandy brown hair lightly oiled and combed back in the style of James Dean, but with none of the wildness. He'd done military duty during the Korean conflict, and still carried himself like a man at perpetual attention, though nearly forty years had passed since the war. His light blue eyes seemed to settle on things without seeing them, and Chester sometimes wondered if his father was still listening for a distant command to call him from what his life had become.

Your father was such a handsome man. He looked like you Chester, but not quite so dark. When Teddy brought him home on leave that time...why I guess it was love at first sight. It was summertime, and Chester was on the couch, listening to his mother, the drawn shades slapping the black screens. The room was in shadows for she was depressed—and sat in semidarkness holding a tumbler of amber whiskey with both hands on her lap. Her eyes were dark brown buttons. She'd cut her dark hair into a short bob and it hung mannishly about her face, which was bloated and doughy from the medications they'd been giving her. *You might not see it now, Chester,* she said, perhaps suspecting what he saw, *but people actually said I was pretty then. I was just, oh, just a slip of a thing, a girl. I didn't know much about the world, but I'd seen enough to suspect there was a whole lot more to it than Cedar Junction. And there was your father smelling of starch in his pressed gray shirt and pants, a breast-full of pins and buttons, his military cap cocked to one side. He was so gentle, so polite. And your father must have thought I was pretty too because he asked me out that very day. "Well imagine that," Teddy said when I told him. Then he just laughed and said "Now you let me know, sis, if old Chester tries anything."*

Young Chester stood in the living room in darkness. The air was fetid and reeked of urine, and he supposed she'd been letting the cats go all over the couch again. All the furniture but the couch had been pushed into a pile in one corner of the living room; the couch, an overstuffed green plaid, reclined at an angle across the middle of the room, facing the blank screen of Zenith television console. Teddy had given it to his mother and father before they got married, just after the war and just before he got killed. She'd never gotten over Teddy's death. *Once a mine almost kissed him in Korea--it missed him by this much,* she said squeezing her fingers together, leaning forward, and the warm, yeasty smell of alcohol on her breath. *And he comes home and a motorcycle kills him. He might have taken Teddy before the war if he was to go that way.* She'd been bitter that day, but other times, during her spells, she'd grow sad and ruminate. *"Maybe He had to take Teddy to make room in the world for you Chet. You were born after he died. Maybe that explains it.*

She closed her eyes, which were cloudy and puzzled, and her mouth frozen somewhere between a grimace and a frown. *Teddy was the only one who ever truly loved me, Chester."*

But he had loved her. He'd been the last one to leave. After his father and younger sister and brother had gotten tired of dealing with her craziness, he had stayed, living at home until he was nearly thirty. He knew what they whispered. Mama's boy. And he knew why they said it. It was the ghost of the malice they felt against themselves. They had left her when the chips were down, and he had stayed. But in the end, even he had left her. It had been impossible to hold a job with her always needing things. Needing something at the store, needing a ride downtown, needing him to stay just a few moments longer. He'd taken a job in a distant county simply as an excuse for parting.

He followed his father into the kitchen where the fluorescent light gave an unnatural pallor to the room. The neighbor stood next to his brother who was ashen, silent and wooden next to the gray Formica kitchen table with its red leather chairs formed on bits of hollow chrome. "Well, you can't live the way she did and survive," the neighbor said. "But what drove her to it? Well, that's between you and God I suppose." His mother was slumped over the stool in an attitude that resembled prayer. And though she was dead and well into middle age, Chester could not divert his gaze from her calves, which still looked shapely and supple beneath her short skirt, as though at any moment she might rise and flounce away. "Chester, you and Art get a bucket and mop from the basement," his father's voice parted the refrigerator's locust hum with strange authority. "I'll call the police." As Chester moved across the kitchen to the basement door, he noticed rigor mort us had set into his mother's hand, which was frozen in a grasping position, and he reminded himself to keep his eyes from her face. He'd run across a dead dog once, and the expression frozen on the dog's face had never left him.

Some relatives came up from Cedar Junction for the funeral. Cousin Bub, a huge shambling, mountain of a man, with a round head and bristly, graying crew cut grasped his father's hand and burst into tears. "I'm sorry, Chet," he said drawing back, eyes red and filmy as onions. He pulled out a huge, white handkerchief to wipe his eyes. Chester stared at the white crew sox that bridged the distance between Cousin Bub's navy suit and his shiny black shoes. "You know she was a cheerleader when I played for the Rebs," Bub said, glancing at his cousin over his shoulder. "I can still see her, plain as yesterday." His father's gaze followed, pale blue eyes still trying to absorb the mystery of how and why such a thing could have happened.

Mrs. Krupps, laid out under the soft yellow lights, for the first time in years wore a peaceful expression. She'd grown her soft, chocolate-colored hair long during the last years of her life, and the undertaker had tied it up in a becoming knot at the back of her head. But he could not disguise the deep lines carved around her mouth, and the ruffled blouse could not hide her thinness, her chest, as flat and narrow as an ironing board beneath the curled crepe. "She was the pride of our family when she went away to that teacher's college, and then marrying a military man." Bub said. "Who would've guessed it would come to this?" He burst into tears again and pressed Chester's hand in both his own, before moving off into a corner.

His mother's chest seemed to heave slightly under the fancy, ruffled blouse. *It always seemed to me Chester, that I was marked, you know, different, somehow special. You know, I was voted most popular girl in my class. Then I went away to teachers' college, and well I just thought the world was my oyster. Maybe it was the sin of pride that finally did me in. But I started doing badly after Teddy died, and then that first student teaching session with all those little children staring up at me like I knew the answers. Well, I didn't know the answers, Chester. I just didn't know them.* She'd run screaming from the classroom and the family had perceived the first signs of her illness. They'd all been relieved when his father had agreed to marry her anyway, and for a long while after that, it had seemed everything would be ok.

He remembered her standing over the green laundry caddy, a ray of dusty sunlight pouring in the basement window. She was folding underwear neatly into thirds, the way his father liked it, and stacking it in piles on top of the dryer. *You know Chester,* she said. *Some day I'd like to fold this underwear in half, just once, mind you, just to see what would happen.* She had mentioned teaching once again, after she sent her last child off to school, and Mr. Krupps had gently reminded her of what had happened the first time. And so, she was silent, keeping house, only getting out to do the shopping, and even stopping that after a while. She complained the neighbors were hostile and unfriendly and that everything looked the same. They'd bulldozed all the trees to make way for the neighborhood and she missed the shade, and despised the dust that the excessive sunlight sent channeling through her house.

I was sick then, I tell you Chester. His mother leaned forward and poked a Lucky Strike in the air at him. Her eyes were bright, and she looked younger than he'd ever seen her. She'd pulled her hair back into a ponytail, but a few strands had escaped the red rubber band. They made her look girlish as she pushed them back with the palm of her hand, still holding the cigarette between two fingers. She pushed the cigarette between puckered lips, snapped a lighter open, lit it, and drew deeply. She'd taken to wearing bright red lipstick, a tube a week, and Chester wondered what the pharmacist must think when he appeared at the counter each Monday asking for Revlon shade number 37 because he was embarrassed to ask for Satin Rouge.

He'd had a friend over that day, and she had cornered the two of them in the living room where they sat drinking her bad coffee and eating Lorna Doone's. *When Chester was growing up, yes that's when I was truly sick. And the minute I started to get better, started to feel good about myself, well his father put me in a hospital. A mental hospital. Look at this, here on my wrist. That's a cigarette burn where one of the inmates got me. You mark my words—Sarah, is it? You watch out for men. As long as they're getting what they want, fine. Clean this and clean that, broil their lamb chops, and fold their underwear. But try and do something for yourself and they turn on you fast as you please. That business in the bible about the garden. That's probably bullshit too.*

Someone had a hand on his shoulder, and Chester saw that the slight movement of his mother's chest had been his imagination. Perhaps he inherited her craziness, and she would have the last laugh yet. But she was dead. As dead as the dog he'd stumbled on in the field that day. His sister had dissolved into tears and now stood red-faced holding the hand of Uncle Bub's wife. Uncle Bub stood wiping his eyes in the corner. His father, and brother, bent over one at a time, and kissed his mother, without emotion, on the cheek. As Chester stared down at his mother, he thought that perhaps her death had happened for the best.

He was remembering the time his mother had first started to come out of her depression—in the early seventies when the family was about to buy a new car. She had wanted Mr. Krupps to buy a red one, a cherry red convertible, and he had refused. He was a creature of habit, and from the day he'd bought his first blue Chevy in 1959 with its sleek tail fins and polished chrome strips, he'd never bought any other color but blue, nor any other make but Chevrolet. "Blue's as good as any other color," he'd said, simply, firmly. "And a convertible is not a family car." But she would not let up. She'd seen the car in a magazine advertisement and talked about it incessantly, day and night, wondering, arguing, cajoling.

When he could not silence her with logic, Mr. Krupps handled the matter as he handled any deviation from normal behavior, by refusing to discuss the matter any further. His lack of emotion had set her off even more, and she carried the battle through the coming weeks, following him one night to the bedroom where he firmly shut the plywood door and locked her out. *I know you can hear me, Chester senior, she shouted through the door. You can shut the door, but you can't shut out my voice. You can't oppress me with your blue cars, and this putrid green house, with all this starch and underwear. I won't have it any more. A red car is all I ask—a convertible to let the air in once in a while. It's not too much.* She shouted for the entire night, her children listening, behind closed bedroom doors. Her voice grew hoarse towards dawn, when the thought that her husband might actually be sleeping through it all nearly drove her mad. It was then she tried to kick the door down. And it was then that Mr. Krupps packed his bags and left her for good.

After that their lives had never really been the same again. Her depression had vanished, but the family had not been prepared for the strange and devastating side effects of the cure. She began moving furniture in crazy ways, haunting local bars, drinking, taking up with entire strangers, talking, talking, and proselytizing to anyone who would listen about the strange, oppressive powers of men. Chester would go to bed with his clothes on, knowing the phone would ring about 1 a.m. when a bartender would call and ask for someone to come pick her up. She drove away those who would tolerate her, and finally, she had driven away the only person who would have loved her. Chester thought of the times he had visited her, and of the times he had stayed away knowing that any time he gave her would not be enough.

His lips brushed her forehead. Powder had settled like dust around the lines and pores of her still face, and for just a moment he wanted to bathe his mother, to wash the silly orange undertaker's mask off her face, to paint his mother's lips a brilliant Satin Rouge. The family was moving toward exit where the shining black limousine waited to swallow their grief with its glinting, smoked windows. Chester stood at the door for a moment, and his gaze swept across the nearly empty parking lot. He saw his father, brother and sister's cars as a smooth, unbroken flash of color on the faded asphalt next to his own new blue Chevrolet.

Vickie A. Carr's work has been published in literary magazines including *Whiskey Island*, *The MacGuffin*, and the *Kansas Quarterly/Arkansas Review* (Transition Issue) and various other literary magazines. An award-winning journalist, she most recently won the Edward R. Murrow Award for a piece she did for NPR. She has taught Creative Writing and Journalism at Curry College, at Pine Manor College, and at the University of Rhode Island. She was a member of the Advanced Creative Writing group at Radcliffe College. She lives by the sea with her husband, her son, and her cat.

Awake
Elaine Terranova

   Last night I dreamed I was awake. An excess of consciousness, maybe. I dreamed I was in a war. Wars now are fought in deserts though how can there be a war in a desert? You have to hide behind trees in a war. Or maybe that's only tag. I dreamed one army was cutting branches from the tree in front of the house and wood was flying through the window. The blanket weighed down my bones. I dreamed there was a sleeping boy in my lap and I couldn't rouse him.

   Elaine Terranova is the author of six collections of poetry, most recently, *Dollhouse*, winner of the Off the Grid Press 2013 Poetry Award. Her poems have appeared in T*he New Yorker, The American Poetry Review, Ploughshares, Prairie Schooner, The Virginia Quarterly Review*, and other magazines, and in such anthologies as, *A Gift of Tongues, Blood to Remember: American Poets Write about the Holocaust*, and *Articulations: The Body and Illness in Poetry*. She has published prose in *Boulevard, South Loop Review, Yaakov Murchada*, and *Frigate*. Forthcoming short stories appear in *Hotel Amerika* and *Per Contra*. She has received a Pushcart Prize, a Pew Fellowship in the Arts, and an NEA Fellowship in Literature.

Not Tonight
Charlotte Snead

She came downstairs with pillow imprints on her cheeks. Her stubborn curls framed her face. She smiled. He wanted her. He always wanted her, but he saw she was still tired. She worked hard in the yard today, and since her back surgery, she felt pain after exertion. He was tired, too, he admitted to himself. Not tonight.

"Whatcha watching?" she asked.

"Just the Germans losing World War II again," he said, repeating her oft-used phrase.

She walked in front of him, threw a leg over his, and lowered herself onto his lap facing him. She leaned against his chest, and his hand curved into her sleep-tousled hair. Their spirits were willing, but their flesh was weak, he thought, holding her to himself and drinking in her scent.

"You wanna watch one of those funny videos?"

"Okay."

"You don't sound too excited," she said

"Neither do you."

She rose and pulled him by the hand. "We'll use the big screen in the other room."

Comfortably settled on the sofa, they clicked the remote until the feature came on. He had his arm around her, but soon they were laughing so hard they drew apart and held hands.

After the first episode finished was over, he needed to tend to some chores. "You got a lot done outside today," he said. "Looks good. You okay?"

"I'll be fine. She stood, her soft cotton gown falling gracefully to her ankles. The plunging neckline left much of her bosom uncovered, and he sighed. He always wanted her. Marriage hadn't changed that. No, it added to it, knowing what they had together, and she never refused him. Sometimes, like now, he wouldn't ask. Just lying next to her, spooned up against her, the warmth of their bodies encircling one another, was enough. It was good.

She wore the soft shift to bed so he couldn't enjoy watching her undress and dress in her nightclothes. He liked to watch her, especially when she had those lacy red panties on—but the black ones were nice, too. Even cotton briefs were good.

She didn't turn her light on to read as she usually did. "I napped, but I'm tired. I was up early cooking for the children. I'm glad they came, but they didn't stay long."

"They have their own lives to lead. But it was a great meal. The turkey was perfect."

"Thanks. I love you."

"I love you, too." He reached over to pat her. He could see the curve of her smile as he leaned against the pillow. So how long have I been loving you now?"

"This December we will have been married forty-nine years. Thank you for loving me."

He reached up and turned off the light. In the darkness he curled his arm around her, took her soft breast in his hand, and replied. My pleasure." It was enough, lying beside the wife of his youth. Another night, when they weren't so tired, but not tonight.

Charlotte and her husband met at Duke University. They have four natural and two chosen children (one adopted and one foster daughter). They have seven grandsons, from adults to a baby. Two more are on the way from China, a boy, 6, and a girl, 12. A pro-life leader for many years, Charlotte believes God creates every child. Four of their grandchildren are adopted. A Phi Beta Kappa graduate of Duke, Charlotte received a Masters of Social Work from the University of North Carolina in 1966. The Sneads live in rural West Virginia. Charlotte's experiences as a wife, social worker, mother, pro-life leader, and mentor of her church's Mothers of Preschoolers chapter contribute to her inspirational fiction.

Empathy
Robin Rosen Chang

He needs her to know with her own calloused hands
the shovel, its metal handle, and the earth's hard jolt
when he thrusts a trowel into dry ground, and how
bones can shudder and break like windows.
He wants her to feel a damaged body's aches
and lopsided gait and its humility when it begs God
for strength to make love to her as if she were a fledgling.

And she longs for him, who comes home when the moon
has almost risen, to realize the sting of giving a depleted body
to a broken man. She needs him to perceive the pinch of a baby
between a narrow pelvis. She prays for him to find and bring
her, just one time, a twig covered with buds that he finds
in a field behind the home where almost nothing grows.

Robin Rosen Chang is an educator and a poet. She has had a career in higher education for many years, teaching composition and other courses in an English as a Second Language Program as well as research methods in the General Education Program at Kean University. Before going into education, she was an urban planner. Her poems have appeared in *WomenArts Quarterly*, *The Paterson Literary Review*, *The Stillwater Review*, *Philadelphia Stories*, and elsewhere. She served as the vice president of South Mountain Poets from 2012 to 2015. She is currently a graduate student in the Warren Wilson College MFA Program for Writers. Robin is a native of Philadelphia and has lived in the Northeast, Southeast, Midwest, West, and overseas.

Eve Strives to Become an Opera Singer

Joanne Leva

She descends and stabilizes
while wading
in the Jordan River.

Nature wraps itself
around woman and bells ring.
Eve decides to renew herself

by purchasing
a ringed binder
with divider sections.

Her dividers are labeled
mind, body and soul.
She envisions

her life a gigantic puzzle
with missing pieces.
She constructs

a circle with strokes
that radiate like brilliant candles,
then tries to write a short story.

Joanne Leva is founder and Editor-in-Chief of *Tekpoet*, an online poetry manuscript services company, which offers a wide array online manuscript services to foster the creative process in developing poetry manuscripts for new and emerging poets.

An advocate for creative writing and community service, Joanne is founder and Executive Director of the Montgomery County Poet Laureate Program. She received the prestigious Philadelphia Writer's Conference Community Service Award in 2011 and serves as President on the Board of Directors for the Indian Valley Arts Foundation.

She has organized poetry readings at Headhouse Square for Earth Day, the Seven Arts Fest on South Street, The Theater of Living Arts, The Philadelphia Museum of Art, The James A. Michener Museum, The Mutter Museum, World Café, and Ambler Theater.

Let Nothing Ye Dismay
or The Eternal Self-Hatred of the
Abused Child's Mind
Robin Black

True understanding rarely arrives as anything whole. The most profound of it comes to us most often in glimmers and in shards, flickers and fragments, information that swirls around, perhaps chaotic, until one day we know something that we didn't know before.

I saw a picture of my father recently, ran into it among old photographs during a recent move. I'm still startled by unexpected images of him, though he died more than twelve years ago. The primitive fear that photographs may steal our souls has this flip-side in experience for me; at the sight of a photograph of my father, I feel the presence of his soul. I feel him flash through me. And then I feel, again, the dizziness of loss. And only then am I steadied to see him. Him. His face.

He looks happy in this picture, leaning up against a window of his old office. Images of my father smiling are ones to which I have a particular response, something like gratitude. See! He could be happy. Here is some evidence of ease and of joy. Despite it all. Despite all the undeniable sadness and all of the fears, there were undoubtedly also these moments of delight.

*   *   *   *   *

In the summer of 2002, just more than a year after my father's death, my husband and I were dining with a close friend, at his seaside home. A congenial trio, we were all the more so that night with the help of a generous supply of alcohol. The grilled steaks were excellent. A fire blazed in the fireplace, and music we could all agree on - Jimmy Buffet singing ballads, to match our seaside locale – hovered in the air.

I don't remember why or how talk turned that night to the subject of religion, though it's a topic that emerges easily enough from me. I have always clung fiercely to my identity as a Half-Southern Methodist/Half-Jew, exercising my prerogative as a self-proclaimed mutt to jettison neither side but maintain instead an idiosyncratic and inherently paradoxical duality of religion inside myself. Fifty-one years old now, I have, *for the most part*, given up trying to persuade anyone that this is no more or less rational than any other religious identity. I have, for the most part, given up. But as I say the topic arises easily enough and there remains a certain defensiveness in me around my right to maintain a sense of Christianity inside myself.

My husband is Jewish, as is my former husband, the father to my two eldest children. For many reasons, not the least of which can be summed up in the phrase *critical mass*, all three of my children have been "raised Jewish," meaning they attended religious school, they have become *Bar* and *Bat Mitvot*.

We were all a little tipsy at that beachside dinner when the subject of my father's Christianity arose. Tipsy enough for me to use the word *Jewthodist* to describe myself and think it very witty, and tipsy enough for our dinner companion, a Jew, to express incredulity at the idea that my father, a man of intellect and in many contexts good sense, well-known for being a logical thinker, believed that Jesus Christ was the son of God. Literally. The actual son. And, perhaps most impressively, tipsy enough for my husband to look amused, rather than terrified as this all too delicate discussion took place.

"Impossible," this friend declared of my father's Christian faith. "He can't actually have thought that God and Mary had a child."

"But he did."

"I don't believe it." Our friend shook his head, as he poured more wine into my glass. "He was too intelligent. It's incomprehensible."

"Okay." I leaned forward, a little heavily from drink. "Here's what I don't understand. I don't understand why once you accept the existence of an all powerful immortal being, of God, why it's any more irrational to think he chose to procreate. Or, for that matter, play golf. The leap, I would think, is between thinking there is a God and not. Not between thinking that there is a God and then thinking he would or wouldn't do this or that. After you accept the existence of God, the rest seems like details to me."

To which my friend replied, "You're absolutely right. I no longer believe in God."

Later, in the remorseful after-glow, my husband assured me that my brilliant, drunken rhetoric hadn't actually robbed a true believer of many decades worth of comforting faith.

"I think he was yanking your chain," he said.

And of course he was right.

So the puzzle that remains for me from this exchange has little if anything to do with my drinking buddy's religious beliefs. The puzzle for me still is why I placed the words "comforting" and "faith" together in a clause, as though it were obvious that they should be linked.

A puzzle, because, as my father's daughter, I had good reason to know better than that.

* * * * *

The fact that my father was a devout Christian was hardly a secret, though he never attended church with any regularity. Nor did he pray at meals or wear a cross around his neck or in any other way wear his religion on his sleeve. But still I knew, while growing up, that he believed. Occasionally, he said so outright. He was prone to declarations of position on matters that mattered to him, and religion was no exception. And there were other signs, unmistakable, and in some cases indisputably odd.

When I was ten, my pet guinea pig died. My father, sparing me the grisly aspects of this death as he could not later do with his own, wrapped the tiny body in a handkerchief and drove it to a garbage can outside the nearby United Methodist Church to deposit it there. Standing over the garbage can, he recited a prayer he had composed on a 3x5 index card: *Dear Lord, Snowball was a sweet, good guinea pig. If there is a guinea pig heaven, I hope and pray you will find a place for her there.* Then he slid this card and a note recounting what he had done under my bedroom door.

The story takes a short detour into comedy here, because for reasons of delicacy my father eschewed the phrase "garbage can" and replaced it with the word "receptacle" the result being that with the willingness of a child to think *anything* possible, I believed for a time that he had put Snowball's rigid rodent corpse in the Goodwill collection box outside the church, and until my mother set me straight, this miscommunication misdirected my understanding of the event and I thought, quite simply, that Dad had done something far too weird to be remotely comforting to me or anyone. But once we cleared up the meaning of the word *receptacle*, I was struck by the reality of the faith that had driven him to do what he did.

He never made any attempt to transmit his belief to my generation. Couples who are of mixed religions can take any of many different paths. My parents chose to incorporate the celebrations of Judaism and Christianity into our home, but not the beliefs. There was no proselytizing from either side – only presents and food: at Christmas, at Passover, at Easter, at Hanukah. Candy canes, matzo balls, chocolate bunnies and chocolate monies, too. But no articles of faith.

Far more conspicuous than my father's religious conviction, was his unhappiness. In my eulogy of him, I described him as "melancholic by nature" and as the word *melancholic* has a purposefully archaic feel to it, so too do other words that might describe his emotional state. *Haunted. Tortured. Tormented.* Woven into my earliest memories is the sight of my father, day after day, sitting in our kitchen, an enormous cup of tea steaming by his side, a pipe hanging from his mouth, his head drooped heavy into his hand, look-ing up to meet my gaze as I approached, rolling his eyes in all too clear pain. Shaken, obviously, by what night had once again delivered unto him.

"I've never had a good night's sleep in my life. I have nightmares, Baby. . ." He would tremble a little, shudder at the memories. "Nightmares so terrible, I won't tell you what they are."

And indeed, he never did, but even so, these nightmares of my father's haunted me. Often, as I lay in my bed, I would hear him rattling in our attic, moving from one room of his office suite to another, unable to sleep. Or unwilling to. Resisting the nightly descent into the horror of his own unconscious being. And I would find my own thoughts drift with the elastic envisioning of a child's sleepy mind into imagining what realm could be so terrifying as to linger over him, diminishing his enjoyment of every follow-ing day.

*   *   *   *   *

Everything we know is made of puzzle pieces scattered, occasionally joined. Only in the joining can we know that the pieces are part of the same puzzle. Only then.

"I've spent every night of my life trying to forgive my parents," he used to say.

At what point did I ask him "forgive them for what?" I'm not sure I ever did, but the story emerged through the years.

"They beat me, baby. They whooped me till I shook."

There was a tree in the yard, he said, and he had been required to select the branches that they used. "It had to be a good one, too. You couldn't try to cheat." There had been alcohol involved, lots and lots of alcohol, and beatings that blended into other beatings until few stood out, distinct. There had been one, though, one so devastating that my father recounted his own father regretting it decades later, as he himself neared death. "We went too far that time. That time it was too much," my father heard his own father say. "That one time we went too far."

Comfort. I believe my father took some comfort from that exchange.

But where my father failed to find comfort, was in his faith.

Hell became a practical problem for our family when we suggested to him, dying then, that he might want to sign a Do Not Resuscitate order, a DNR. He was eighty-four years old and riddled with so many illnesses that when I asked my mother, "Is there anything Dad doesn't have?" her answer was, "Only teeth."

The disease that got him in the end was a rare form of skin cancer that itself carried a whiff of myth to it, a cautionary tale about the futility of out-running one's own history. Ancient mistakes, unknown as such at the time, can lurk, later to emerge from our own narratives, fatal finally. The cancer appeared as he passed eighty, first on his nose, barely noticeable. But those small patches grew, devouring his skin, ultimately causing the disintegration of that feature, and indeed much of his face, working its way through him like a singularly malicious curse – though the true origin was x-ray treat-ments he had received for acne, given in the late 1920's or early 30's.

My father's reaction to the suggestion of a DNR was simple and shock-ing all at once. He wanted to talk to a Catholic priest. He wanted to know if signing would be tantamount to suicide and would result in his being damned to Hell. He wasn't a Catholic – he had always balked at the doctrine of Papal infallibility – but he wanted the strictest possible reading of the rules, and he wasn't taking any chances with the Methodists.

The priest who appeared assured him that even the Catholics have no problems with DNR's, and the document was signed. So that was the end of that. Except of course that it wasn't the end for me - because of what I'd learned.

Hell.

Hell is a metaphor to me. It is the act of imagining unimaginable pain. It is paintings I have seen, words that I have read. It is the idea of something being as bad as one can imagine; and then worse than that. It is a rhetorical device, a challenge to the imagination, a fear tactic; and not a real place. Hell does not exist for me.

But it did exist for my father. That was what I learned. Hell was an all too real possibility, drawing ever closer in the months before his death.

It comes back again to the question of why somebody else's religious be-liefs can seem *unbelievable*. As the priest came and left, and my father's nurse witnessed the mark that he made on the page, it was unbelievable to me that my father was worried - as one worries about some practical issue like running out of gas or whether the milk is fresh - about eternal damnation.

During those final months, the Fall of 2000, early 2001, my father hov-ered between lucidity and delusion. All of the faculties that are likely to fail, did. The bladder, the bowels, the brain. He lost track of time and of place, lost his knowledge of who each of us was - and then knew everything again for days at a time. The physical, the emotional, the spiritual, past, present, the unimaginable future; all are loosely joined, reconfigured, in slow and certain death.

I have wondered, writing this, whether I care when the pieces fell together for me, when I gained an understanding of my father's lifelong sleepless nights, but I have decided it doesn't matter whether it was before or after the stroke he had that December, whether it was while I was in the room with him, perched beside him on his bed, or miles away, cooking dinner, in my own home. All that matters is that as my father's reality fell into fragments, certain shards of it reassembled, inside of me.

There was a conversation in his room. I used to say of Dad's study, where he spent his final illness and where he died, that it was the externalization of his *Id*. The space was crowded, bursting to overflow with his artwork, his books, his trumpet, souvenirs of travels with my mother, pictures of us all, drawings by his grandchildren. Even the smells – turpentine, tobacco, urine – competed for space, overlapping and creating new versions of themselves. When I describe myself as "my father's daughter," when I find the connection that a child naturally seeks, part of what I locate is this odd combination of clarity and chaos that has always resided within us both. Certain corners of his study would reveal themselves to be orderly, files alphabetized, aspects of his work recorded perfectly. But the overall impression was that a none too careful ransacking had occurred.

We were sitting on his bed, our feet dangling over the side, his, feeble and swollen twice their healthy size. And of course we were smoking. After more than seventy years of puffing away, my father had gratefully reached an age and stage at which everyone had stopped nagging him to stop. I haven't smoked for years and never did very much, but always did around him – another sought connection, perhaps. By the time this conversation took place, he had grown too weak to grasp a cigarette, so I held one in each of my hands, placing his between his lips as I took a drag from my own.

My father had a lifelong habit of speaking from the train of his own thoughts, as though the listener had been privy to them and could easily join in. "I have tried and I have failed," he said to me.

"To do what?"

"I cannot forgive those two people. But baby, I have done nothing but try."

"Dad, it's understandable. . ."

He shook his head. "Honor thy father and mother," he said to me. "So commands the Lord. And I cannot. Baby, I have failed."

My father had a face that could express a depth of sadness defying measurement. The light brown of his eyes seemed to come from a palette mixed purposefully for the depiction of grief. And as this conversation occurred, that face had already been ravaged by disease. The smoke that he inhaled, he exhaled through only vestiges of what had been a beautiful, even noble nose.

In his final months he seemed more ancient than merely old.

But speaking of his parents then, he became a boy again. Childhood visited his being, catching up with him in the end, so I could see him, clearly, see who he was to himself. Somebody's son.

I didn't know what to say. I told him something I believed but that I don't think helped him at all. I said that he was misreading the fifth commandment – giving it too strict an interpretation to make any logical sense. "I think that by devoting your life to trying to forgive your parents for what they did, you *have* honored them," I said. "It can't mean never dishonor your parents, never feel anger at them – because if it does, we're all guilty for all our lives. If it does, it's just an impossible commandment to fulfill."

But nobody can define for anyone else what they believe. This has been my position all along. Nobody can convince me that it is impossible to be both Jewish and Christian at the same time. And I was not able to talk my father out of the conviction that he had let down his God.

Was he still alive when I understood that this was what kept him up at night for all those years? I don't know. The logic of it, the poetry of it too, fell gradually on me, until I knew it was those intimations of Hell that filled his dreams, the Hell that he feared would welcome him at his death, because he had not been able to forgive his parents for abusing him, for making him choose the branches that they used, for taking turns at whooping him until he shook.

Somewhere in the heart of every abused child lies the suspicion that he or she deserves the abuse. The abused child who fathered me was no exception to this rule, and at the intersection of emotion and of faith, he devised an unimaginably terrible punishment for himself.

My father has been gone for more than twelve years now. And I often wonder why I cling with such tenacity and against the tide of my own household to a religion that I believe brought him such extraordinary pain. It might be more logical, more sensible, to disavow what caused someone I love those thousands upon thousands of nightmare-filled nights.

But then there are those words before me on the page: *Logical. Sensible. Religion. Believe.* And I should know better by now than to try to pull these particular puzzle pieces together into a rational whole. I should know better than to seek in logical argument an alternative to being who I am: the daughter who herself fought sleep as a child, listening to his footsteps, fearing that his nightmares might mingle with my own. The daughter who cannot ever disentangle or disavow his half of me.

He is buried near my house and when I visit him, I talk to him. And at times I pray – in my own way. I pray for my father to have found the peace I never doubt that he deserves. I pray for the shattered little boy he was to be somehow healed. But I haven't recorded my prayers on a 3x5 index card, to slip under the door of a grieving child. I have written this instead.

Robin Black is the author of the story collection, *If I loved you, I would tell you this*, the novel, *Life Drawing*, and most recently *Crash Course: Essays From Where Writing and Life Collide*. She lives with her family in Philadelphia.

Memories of Peaches
Beth Moulton

They capture the sun of high summer,
all reds and golds and sticky warmth,
and their fragrance stirs a blood memory
of things I've never learned but always knew.
The knowledge of my mother and her mother,
and generations before,
who had to save the sun of summer
for winter's stingy light.

As the sweet aroma fills the room,
they come to me –
these women who share my blood
and my need to hold back the dark.
I see my eyes in their eyes,
feel their hearts in my chest,
their hands guide mine.
I am cradled in an unending line of woman
as we labor together to preserve the sun.

During the dying times ahead,
as I savor small bites of summer,
These women will come again.
I have preserved their memory,
Along with these peaches,
To nourish myself through winter.

Beth Moulton is an MFA candidate at Rosemont College. She has been published in *Bartleby Snopes*, *A Clean, Well-Lighted Place*, *scissors and spackle*, and *Circa, A Literary Review*. She lives and works near Valley Forge, PA with her two cats, Lucy and Ethel.

Short Order, Long Time

Mara Buck

"One order of rich and famous life coming right up." The waitress with the beehive hair scribbles on a 'guest check' pad, using a pen proclaiming *Good Eats*. The pen is on a retractable cord that when released springs back to dangle just below her name tag. Betty, reads the name tag. Frank's crooning on the box, something about being seventeen. There are crackers in a red plastic basket. I'm hungry, but not for crackers.

I drum my fingers on the formica. It's been a paralyzing wait for a simple order. "Excuse me." I flag down a waitress. "Could you ask Betty how much longer it'll be for my rich and famous life? I've been waiting quite a while."

"Betty? She died two years ago. I'll check in the kitchen." This one's a "Tammy" with a pixie cut and she stuffs a Bic into her pocket. She refills the crackers in the basket. Is that David Bowie in the background?

The springs in the vinyl seat of the booth are drilling into my increasingly boney bottom. For the sake of all that's holy, why is this taking so long? I've seen others come and go and yet here I sit. The Saltines have been replaced with Triscuits, Bowie has morphed into Lady Gaga, and yet here...

"Excuse ME! I've been waiting, like forever, you know and do you, like you know, have my order coming up real soon? A plate of rich and famous life? A la carte? Nothing on the side, but you know, like, some water would be like, you know, okay?" I'm trying to communicate in the language style of those around me, but I'm falling woefully short. The latest server is named Beryllium and I think my eyes are a tad woozy, because I can't tell if it's a she or a he. There's a swatch of tie-dyed hair and tattoos and its face is sprouting gold rings from all manner of painful spots. He/she rolls red-pencilled eyes and punches in a succession of keys on a plastic gadget. There's still music in the background, but it's as unrecognizable as static. A great deal of hair has accumulated on the table in front of me. It's gray and stringy and I do believe it may be mine.

"Ready for pickup for table seventy. One order of rich and famous life."

A robotic hand sets the plate before me. There seems to be a great deal of green fuzzy mold and a spider eyes me accusingly as she protects the strands of her web. Screw the mold. Fuck the spider. I dig in and it's as delicious as I had always anticipated.

Mara Buck writes, paints, and rants in a self-constructed hideaway in the Maine woods. She has won awards or been short-listed by the Faulkner/Wisdom Society, the Hackney Awards, Carpe Articulum, Maravillosa, The Binnacle. Her work has appeared in *Huffington Post*, *Crack the Spine*, *Blue Fifth*, *Pithead Chapel*, *Writing Raw*, *The Tishman Review*, *The Maine Review*, *Apocrypha and Abstractions*, *The Linnet's Wings*, *Poets for Living Waters*, *Orion*, *The Lake*, and others, as well as in numerous print anthologies. A portfolio from her gallery-sized installation was published in *Drunken Boat* with other art showcased in *Scientific American* online. Her art, poetry, and video appear on the site of the World Trade Center Memorial. Current projects include a novel and a collection of strange stories of Maine.

Happy Anniversary
Tori Bond

He pointed to the chart of the inverse relationship in our relationship. He drew his finger seductively along the time horizon. It represented time spent together.

Linear time? I asked.

Time is always linear, he said, can't be anything but linear. He liked to be exact.

I begged him not to be so literal to which he said, how else would one talk about charts? I asked total hours? Or simply time past?

He claimed that all time was past, his voice annoyed.

I claimed present and future as time. He said we were talking about our relationship not verb tenses. I found it interesting that he mentioned verbs since there were so few of them in our relationship.

Exactly! He pointed at the diagonal purple line.

Is this about sex?

No, he said and stabbed the chart with his finger, time-past increased infrequency of sex.

I corrected him, you mean frequency. He preferred to use negative terms to talk about negative things. He did not like to be corrected.

Desire is a complex equation, I said.

It was a simple chart why could I not understand, he shouted.

I asked where was the jagged red line of resentment? How about the scatter plot of loneliness points across an Adirondack sky? There needs to be a Depression Era plummet line of communication. What about the empty pie charts of affection? You forgot to diagram the twins in lovely shades of Venn. His eyes went dead, that would be a circle, he said. I declared his chart meaningless. He assured me charts don't lie.

Tori Bond's short fiction has appeared in *Flash Fiction Funny* anthology, *Monkey Bicycle*, *Extraordinary Gifts* anthology, *Nailpolish Stories* Best of 2013 Issue, and others. She received honorable mention in the Flash Fiction Chronicles String-of-10 FIVE Flash Fiction Contest, and the 76th Annual *Writer's Digest* Writing Competition. Tori earned an MFA in Creative Writing from Rosemont College and during her time there she was the flash fiction editor for *Rathalla Review*. Tori is co-editor for the serial novel *Naked Came the Cheesesteak* with *Philadelphia Stories* and is currently working on a satirical novel. When not locked in a room writing, chauffeuring kids to endless social engagements, or patrolling the make-out palace formerly-known-as-the-basement, you can find Tori wandering around in the woods.

Beyond Polite Conversation
Dawn Lowe

I raised my son Derek to be polite, and when he decided to kill himself, he did it in a most considerate fashion.

Derek was a teaching assistant at the University of Wisconsin who waited until after the summer session to end his life so as not to inconvenience his students. On August 16, after his last payday, he left $620 in his apartment to pay clean-up costs for the damage he was about to do.

In his suicide note, entitled I'm So Sorry, Derek apologized for not having time to cancel his gas, electrical or cable services, but left enough money to pay outstanding bills. He had emptied and cleaned the refrigerator.

I can't imagine what Derek was thinking as he sponged out the empty vegetable drawer of his refrigerator.

I do know that later that evening, he put on a suit and tie and drove his Chevy Malibu to Fleming's Steakhouse where he bought the most expensive dinner on the menu, washed down with cognac. He scraped the passenger side of his car backing out of a parking structure as he drove home.

When he arrived back at his apartment he filled a fancy brandy snifter with more cognac and took a last photo of himself, his hair tousled and his eyes glassy from the effects of too much alcohol. He left this photo on his desk for police identification.

He had already prepared a suicide note, signed and dated, and left other important documents in a folder on his desk. When he felt ready, he wedged the refrigerator against the door, sat in the bathtub and shot himself in the head.

I learned most of these details from Dr. Sean Tate, the Madison, Wisconsin, Medical Examiner. The ME insisted that I call him Sean, and when my husband and I flew to Madison to claim Derek's body, rather than asking us to meet him at the morgue, Sean came to our hotel.

After shaking hands in the lobby, Sean suggested that we talk in the hotel restaurant, decorated in a sports theme honoring the University of Wisconsin Badgers. The walls and carpet were done up in the team colors of red and white: Blood and bone, I thought. Against this backdrop, we ordered cups of tea.

My husband and I slid into one side of a booth, while Sean hoisted his bulk onto the other, placing his black briefcase on the table. He was a melancholy Santa Claus of a man with white hair and beard.

"I'm sorry for your loss," he began, taking my measure. He opened the briefcase and studied my face again. "I brought the suicide note and some of

Derek's possessions."

Under the table, my husband reached for my hand. Feeling tears start to come, I pushed his hand away and forced myself to concentrate.

Reaching into the briefcase, Sean produced the suicide note, Derek's apartment and car keys, his passport and credit cards, all of which were sealed in plastic bags as if to protect us from catching something by touching them. I ripped open the bag with the note, read it silently and passed it to my husband, wiping away tears. I hated crying in front of the waitress, who stared at the items on the table when she walked past.

"Your husband is not Derek's father?" Sean asked me.

"No," my husband Doug answered quickly. "Derek's father died nine years ago from cancer. We've been married five years."

"Can I see my son's body?" I asked Sean.

Sean sipped his tea and shook his head. "The body is not suitable for viewing."

"I don't care," I said. "I want to say goodbye to Derek." Doug tried again to grip my trembling hand under the table and again I pushed him away.

Sean cleared his throat and nervously tapped his fingers on the table. "I don't think you should see Derek's body. You couldn't even hold his hand, you see, because his of decomposition; his fingertips had begun to disintegrate."

Sean appeared sad and a bit reproachful, when I'd forced him to take off his mask and discuss the true nature of his job. I looked away from him at the red walls over his head and silently gave up any hope of seeing Derek's body. I reached for Doug's hand under the table.

"Can I at least see Derek's apartment?" I asked Sean.

He seemed relieved that discussion of the body had been dropped. "I don't see why you couldn't visit the apartment, but let me call the landlady to make sure." Flipping open his mobile phone, Sean punched in some numbers and started to talk. "Listen, I have Mom and Dad here and they want to see Derek's apartment … It's all right, isn't it? Great."

Derek had been 24 years old and a self-reliant adult for six years, and the Mom and Pop familiarity Sean used to describe us in his phone conversation felt insulting. Sean didn't know Derek, Doug, or me at all, and yet, he controlled every moment of this painful situation.

"We're all set," Sean told us. "My car's outside, and I can drive you to the apartment. We have Derek's keys to open the door," he added, picking them out of the pile of personal effects lying on the table. I scooped up the rest of Derek's things and held them protectively, taking care that the edges of the suicide note weren't creased.

Doug and I climbed into Sean's Ford Escort and we drove three blocks to the building where Derek had lived during his last year of life. I had never seen the inside of his apartment.

The previous Christmas, I'd stayed a week at the Best Western hotel in Madison visiting Derek, and during that time my son had never invited me inside his apartment. In retrospect I see that Derek rarely invited me inside any of his private places.

When Doug, Sean and I arrived at Derek's apartment we found a sheet of heavy plastic with a zippered opening taped over the door. Sean unzipped the plastic barrier and used Derek's key.

Behind the door we found a wheezing metal robot with transparent sides. Plastic hoses protruded from either side of the robot's chest; one hose extended backward into the bathroom and the other forward through an open window. The gasping robot pulled contaminated air from the bathroom and replaced it with fresh air from outside the building every few minutes.

Derek's clothes lay on top of his bed. I grabbed one of his T-shirts and held it to my face, hoping to catch his familiar scent. I inhaled deeply, but the shirt was saturated with the odor of strong chemicals used to disinfect a place where a dead body had lain decomposing for three days. I replaced the shirt on the bed, bitterly disappointed.

Sean said, "You can take anything you want from the apartment; we don't need any evidence. The landlady will have the Salvation Army to pick up the rest."

Looking around, I found the suitcase I'd given Derek for a graduation gift and popped it open. There were so few things to put inside: Derek's backpack, some photos, a high-tech umbrella that wouldn't break in the wind. Derek had told me how much he liked this umbrella and now I handled it as if it were an irreplaceable relic.

Doug and I left the apartment within a half hour; it smelled bad, and Derek had left little for us to examine. Sean drove us back to our hotel where he handed me a list of contact details for local funeral homes.

"You need to call a funeral director," Sean told me, indicating one that charged the lowest fee for cremation, which Derek had requested in his suicide note.

Sean was obviously keen to make sure I called a funeral director and listened as I made the call.

"Can I watch the cremation?" I asked the funeral director.

"We can do that," the funeral director replied hesitantly, "but it will delay the process for two weeks."

I told the funeral director to forget it. I wanted Derek's body removed from the morgue right away, and I didn't want to stay any longer than necessary in the cheerful university town of Madison where I saw so many smiling young men.

When I'd set a meeting with the funeral director and put away my mobile phone, Sean handed me his business card and said goodbye. "If there's anything more I can do to help, please don't hesitate to call," he said. But I didn't. I never wanted to see him again.

Since my son's death, I've come to prefer brutal honesty to polite superficiality. When Derek reached adulthood and left home we had polite conversations, but nothing more. I didn't want to be the prying mother and he hated asking me for money. Derek approved my remarriage to Doug but wasn't fond of his stepfather.

When Doug and I were in Madison, we shopped at Target. I looked across the street and saw Fleming's Steakhouse where Derek ate his last meal.

"Look. There's Fleming's," I told Doug, who burst into tears.

"I wish I had known him better," Doug sobbed in my arms as gawking university students streamed around us on the sidewalk.

"So do I," I replied. I had a dream in which a stranger showed me a piece of paper bearing the words You really didn't know him at all.

My husband and I drove Derek's battered Chevy to five car dealers before convincing one of them to buy it for $50. Derek had emptied the car except for some cassette tapes and a tube of Chapstick he'd dropped on the floor that is now one of my most prized possessions.

Derek's friends created a Facebook page in his memory bearing the admonition that contributors should "keep it clean and polite" for my sake. I wish they hadn't.

Derek was my only child and I am no longer a mother. My motherhood was stolen from me overnight and all the unpleasant details of that theft were tidied up before I arrived on the scene---and so his death remains unreal to me.

Some of my relatives have spread the word that Derek shot himself accidentally, and I know they have good intentions. But I am striving for a more honest, messier and less comfortable future.

Writing this story is the first step I've taken in that direction.

Dawn Lowe, 61, has dual American/Irish citizenship and lives north of Dublin on the Irish seacoast. She is the editor and publisher of *Brilliant Flash Fiction*, an online magazine, and attends weekly meetings of the Sapphire Writers' Group at the Irish Writers' Centre in Dublin. In 2008, she returned to school after a 30-year absence to earn a Master's Degree in English Language Teaching and worked as a volunteer helping Irish immigrants. She turned to creative writing as therapy after the death of her son Derek in 2011.

Her work has been broadcast on RTE Radio 1 Sunday Miscellany and published in *Boyne Berries 2013-2014*, *Three Monkeys Online*, *Literary Juice*, and *Clebran*. She plays piano and thinks up stories while walking on the beach.

Apple Girl

J.V. Foerster

My grandmother's house always smelled
like apples. Apple kuchen, applesauce,
apple peels. Sweet smell of her soft home.

My mother hated the smell of apples.
My grandma confessed it was
because when she was pregnant with my mother
she climbed the apple trees and ate the tiny green
apples before they were ripe,

The village women stirred up a storm about
that young farmer's wife full with her first child
being crazy and barefoot up those trees.

Among the gentle mother apple trees
cool green hands in the summer's heat.
A young girl clutching the pearls of green in her apron
sneaking them home to eat them with salt.

I always believed it was the seeds
a tiny seed that planted itself deep in her body.
Warm, snug the fetus grew and grew
drinking for nine months
the nectar of sour green apples.

Tired of the culture of apples my mother
came out 12 pounds with screaming fists of insanity
bearing apple leaves sticky with juice.

J.V. Foerster has been published for over 20 years in various literary magazines and journals, including: *Eclectica*, *Agnieszka's Dowry*, *Red River Review*, *Midnight Mind*, *Premiere
Generation Ink*, and *Women Writers Online* to name just a few. She was also privileged to be
nominated in 2011 for a Pushcart for her work in *Fox Chase Review*. J.V. has been a judge
for the Oregon Poetry Society and has been a mentor to many young poets. She is a pho-
tographer and painter and has had work published in online magazines as well has taken
part in gallery shows. J.V. lives in Brightwood, Oregon in a rain forest on the Sandy River
with ravens, crows and Mr. Buttons the Aussiedoodle.

Blue Smell of Steel
Tery Aine Griffin

The clock on top of the TV says ten; Luke told Olivia to be in by midnight. She'll be late, he thinks. Some nights he looks out the window, half expecting to find her sitting outside checking her watch to be sure, just to be very sure, she's not in by whatever time he named. "That kid, Maria," he says to the TV, "that kid, she don't listen like she used to." He grabs the remote, punches the seek button. The cowboy flick turns into a car commercial then a heavy man in an old-time baseball uniform appears, standing at home plate, tapping the ground before him with his bat. Luke shakes his head, swings his legs off the couch. Well, if I ain't here, he thinks, then I don't know she's late. He feels his tee shirt pocket, looks around, retrieves a pack of Marlboros from the floor beside the couch. I don't know she's late, we don't have to fight about it. He tosses the remote onto the couch, stands and stretches, grunts as his fingers touch the ceiling and his backbone cracks. Bad enough we'll have to fight about the other. He lights a Marlboro, stashes pack and matches in his pocket. Olivia and her damned university. He decides to head out to the Riverside. Like she's some kind of big-shot's kid; I'm surprised she don't want to go to the fancy college near the river. Well, she's a minor. She'll have to do what I say. He takes a long drag off the cigarette, then reaches over and pushes dead butt-ends out of the way as he crushes the cigarette in the ashtray. The law is on my side in this, he thinks. She'll see.

Luke's blue Dodge jumps as the engine catches. Luke pumps the gas pedal, and the pickup sputters. He sees Darling's face, Oliver Darling sitting next to him in an army-green troop truck lurching through the morning fog. "Faggot name," he says. Darling had been snoring lightly. Luke was thinking about Maria, about her belly, which had not begun to swell, not yet. They'd decided the Saturday before Luke left: it would be Luke, Jr. if it was a boy, Olivia if not. Luke had closed his eyes and dreamed of the taste of a steak house dinner. Then his head banged against the wall as the troop truck stopped. He opened his eyes expecting, almost, to see Maria. It was his goddamn first anniversary, and he was supposed to be home, taking Maria out to dinner, and then going home and getting laid. His goddamn first anniversary, and he had to spend it cramped into a troop truck, then standing like an idiot with a gun they wouldn't let him use, not really, not here. And because of what? Because of a bunch of goddamn… "Move out," he heard. He saw Darling, unfolding in a mass of olive green. As the tailgate dropped open, Luke was surprised to hear birds sing.

Now Luke buries Darling's face in the roar of the engine as he slams his pickup truck's pedal to the floor. It was one morning. It was a long time ago. And he doesn't want to think about it now.

"Here's the guy you want," Harvey says as Luke pushes through the door at the Riverside. Luke looks around the bar to see who Harvey's talking to. Old Matthew in his usual place on the last stool. Two girls halfway around the bar. They are older than Olivia, too old even for the fancy college. Maybe just rented an apartment in the neighborhood. Have to check them out later. A kid with slicked-down hair sitting in front of the pickled eggs. Black guy in mechanic's blues near the door. You better stay near that door, Luke thinks. Used to be we'd chase the likes of you the hell out of here. Bastard.

"Usual?" Harvey asks. Luke nods. "Luke was in the Guard. Rumor has it he shot him some commies. Luke, tell the kid about the Guard."

The kid turns to Luke. Luke walks down the bar and sits halfway between the kid and the girls. He tosses his cigarettes on the bar and takes the bottle of Miller Harvey has set in front of him. He looks at his own image reflected above the line of tequila bottles. Cuervo Gold. He'll have a shot later. Tastes good, with a beer chaser. Luke told Harvey about it once, about catching someone in your sights, pulling the trigger, watching him fall 'til he hit the ground. Bragged about it. Thought it would be good for a couple free drinks. He's sick of it now. He wishes Harvey wouldn't tell that damned story anymore.

"Shit." Luke turns to the kid, looks at the kid's hair. What do they call that? Greasers? No, that was the sixties; they got to call it something else now. He spins the Miller so the label faces the kid, then tilts the bottle toward him as if it were a restaurant wine. "Harvey tell you he keeps his beer at fifty degrees, right on the nose?"

The kid opens and closes a book of matches that says "Make Good Money – Drive a Truck" on the cover. "Yeah. So?"

"Perfect temperature for beer." The kid is wearing blue jeans, and a Red Sox jacket over a black tee shirt with something written on it. Luke can't make out the words. "You from the college?"

"Me?" The kid shakes his head. "No."

"You got a name?"

"David. David DeAngelo." David closes the matchbook cover and tosses the matches into an ashtray.

Luke studies the label on his beer. "Well, Dave, the thing is that people don't think temperature matters with beer, but it does. It's too cold, you can't taste it. Too warm, tastes like piss." Luke sips his beer. "Now this, this is perfect."

"You were in the Guard?"

"I was in the Guard."

"What kind of stuff did you do?"

"Guard's good shit, Dave."

David rolls his glass between his palms. "I been thinking about joining."

Luke drinks. "You be glad you ain't one of them college kids." He sees jackets of camouflage, jackets of army drab. "Bunch of goddamn hippies."

"What kind of stuff did you get to do?"

"Stuff. You know. Guard the home front. Lot of people, lot of people meant this country harm." They passed before his sights. Hair like jungle animals. "Lot of them looked like that guy," shaking his head toward the black man near the door. "Screaming about their goddamn equal rights. Like they ain't already got it better than us suckers that work for a living, huh?" Luke takes a Marlboro from the pack and lights it. "Off in colleges, the bunch of them, and you know who was paying for it? You know who? Me, that's who. With my goddamn taxes from my first body-work job." He raises the Miller and takes a long drink. "And the rest of them. Bunch of boys looking like a bunch of goddamn girls. Hair down to their asses. Stoned out on dope all the time." Each one looked like the one before and the one behind. "Well, not all of us were goddamn long-haired ... goddamn ... shit."

He touches his chest where the rock had hit, bruising him through his riot gear. "Someone had to stop the bastards." Some son of a bitch, he'd thought. "Like they say, it's your country. Love it or get the hell out, you know?" Some son of a bitch had hit him. "Some son of a bitch ...." He inhales, then aims a stream of smoke at his beer bottle's neck. Curve of the trigger against his finger. "Gimme another beer, Harvey. Give Dave a beer, too. Looks like a good kid. On me."

Harvey pops the caps off two Millers and sets them on the bar. "How's that kid of yours, Luke? She still home?"

"What, Olivia? Shit. She got some idea in her head about going to that Jefferson State University. Don't know what's the matter with her. I told her, study for a secretary, maybe for a nurse. Nurse'd be handy when she has kids, you know? But no, not Olivia. She wants to run off wild somewhere. It's that damn friend of hers, that Christine. What Christine does, Olivia got to do. Well, I told her and I'll tell you, I'll tell you, too—she's got another think coming."

David takes a long sip of his beer. "Did you really shoot somebody? Did they die?"

Luke drains his beer, reaches for the second. "Nobody, kid." Morning-cool rain had touched his fingers. Cool rifle barrel cradled in his palm, butt against his shoulder, blue smell of polished steel. "Nobody worth a damn." Camouflage jacket, dark curls, books filled his sights. "You'll never hear me say I'm sorry either, kid. You'll never hear me say that."

Home later, Luke grabs a can of Budweiser from the fridge, then bangs on Olivia's bedroom door. "Why you wanna go that place anyway?" talks to the closed door. Tries it to find it locked. "Why you wanna go there?" She's just pretending to be asleep. He's sure of it. "I wanna talk to you, you hear?" He punches the door. "You hear me?" He punches the wall outside his own bedroom, then slams his bedroom door.

In the morning, Luke gets the newspaper off the stoop and walks into the kitchen. He reads the headline: "Students burn flag." "Shit. It don't change."

A pipe bangs as Olivia turns on the water upstairs. Luke pours a mug of black coffee, sits at the kitchen table, lights another smoke. He hears footsteps on the staircase. Olivia shuffles in. He doesn't recognize the pants she's wearing, but he's seen the Jefferson State sweatshirt before.

"Look here," Luke says, waving the front page. "It don't change. It don't ever change."

Olivia takes the milk container out of the fridge, examines it, frowns. "How come you buy this? The one percent is better."

Luke flattens the newspaper against the table. "You want something else, you go buy it."

She pours herself a glass.

"What time you get in last night? You in before midnight, like I said?"

"What time did you get in?"

"I'm the grown-up. You're the kid. What I do is none of your business."

"Yeah, well … " Olivia ducks back into the fridge, roots around, comes out with a slice of pizza. "You'll have to do dinner. I won't be home. I'm going to check out the Jefferson State campus today."

Luke lowers his mug onto the Formica kitchen table and runs his palm across the mug's rim. "What do you want to go there for?" He cups his hand over the mug, studies the place where his wedding ring used to be. Damn it, Maria, he thinks. There are times when I could really use for you to be here. He slides his hand back down the side of the mug.

"It's not too hard to get into, Dad." Olivia takes a bite of the pizza. "And it's cheap."

Luke looks up from his coffee. "What's wrong with the community college? It's ten minutes up the road. You can start there."

Olivia finishes her milk, takes the glass over to the sink, runs water over it. "I don't want to go to the community college."

Luke watches her rinse the glass. It could be Maria: dark curls falling over slender shoulders, one last shake of the glass before she sets it in the drain-board. He wonders what Maria would think if she could see this younger version of herself, of the way she looked when he met her. He feels, for a moment, as if Maria were nearby.

"The art program at the community college sucks," Olivia says.

"Art ... I used to know a guy named Art," Luke recalls. "Little Jewish guy." He pictures the three of them lined up in the drill room at headquarters: Darling, Luke, Art. Then lined up on damp grass, Art, Luke, Darling, standing at ease, gun butts planted in a close-mown campus lawn, barrels pointed toward God. "Named his rifle after some kind of Hebrew warrior. What the hell do you want to learn art for? What're you gonna do with that?"

"Daddy, we've been over this. I hate typing and blood makes me puke. I want to study art. My teachers say I'm good at it. I have an eye."

"What would your mother say, you still a kid and running off to live in another state?"

"I'm not a kid. It's only a two-hour drive. And my mother's dead."

Luke slumps back in his chair. "Your mother's dead, all right." God knows, he thinks, maybe she could do something with you. He smells his cigarette filter burning, crushes the butt into the pile in the ashtray. "Who's going to take care of you way the hell out there?"

"I'm almost eighteen, Dad. I can take care of myself." Olivia takes a hairbrush from her pocketbook, tosses her hair over one shoulder, starts to brush. "Anyway, it's a college campus. How much trouble can I get into there?"

Luke's fingers press hard against his mug. "You don't know nothing about it," he says. "You think you know all about it, all of you kids, but you don't know nothing. It ain't what you think out there. People out there ... people got knives ... people got guns." Art had been comfortable with his rifle.

"Oh, for God's sake."

Comfortable, comfortable, comfortable. Luke was not comfortable, with the rifle butt buried in the grass. He listened, listened for the order.

A car horn sounds outside the window.

"That's Christine," Olivia says. She opens the fridge, grabs another piece of pizza and a Coke. "Gotta go."

"Olivia."

"It's just for the day, Dad. Just to look around." She walks toward the door. "I'll be back late." The door slams behind her.

Luke follows her, stops at the living room window and stares out. "You can't go there," he shouts. Christine's old blue Chevy is in the driveway. "I can stop you." He reaches for a cigarette, bumps against a vase of dead flowers on the shelf. He sees a long flower stem sliding into Darling's rifle. A girl is smiling. Luke stands stiff, still. Feels Art—to his right—grow tense. Sees grass, sees buildings, sees nothing. Girl. Long daisy stem slides into Luke's rifle. "Peace." Cool steel in his hand, rifle barrel hard against clenched fingers. Fingers reaching for daisy pulling it grinding it grinding it face tense, and he shoves the vase back against the wall. Olivia strolls across the lawn, eating pizza, waving to Christine.

Rifle butt smooth against hand, smooth against shoulder through shirt. "I can stop you," he whispers.

Birds sing. Blue smell of polished steel.

Left eye closes, right eye against sights. Morning-cool rain touches fingers. They pass before his sights, hair like jungle animals. He listens, listens for the order. Love it or leave it. They pass; some look at him; some do not.

Rock against chest. Some. Finger. Son of a. Books fill sights. Bitch. Camouflage fills sights. Trigger. Noise. Shoulders fill sights. Dark curls fill sights. Shoulders fill sights. Dark curls fill sights. Shoulders fill sights. Dark curls fill sights.

Olivia, laughing, ducks into the campus-bound car.

Tery Griffin was born in Connecticut and has been a Delaware resident since 2006. She holds an MFA in Creative Writing from the University of Michigan, where she won a Hopwood Major Short Fiction Award. Her fiction has appeared in literary journals including *ninepatch*, *Men As We Are*, *O. Henry Festival Stories* and *The Wittenberg Review*, among others. In 2010, Tery was awarded an Individual Artist Fellowship in Fiction, from the Delaware Division of the Arts. She was chosen as a fiction fellow in the Cape Henlopen Writers' Retreat, sponsored by the Delaware Division of the Arts and the Delaware State Arts Council, in both 2008 and 2014. She lives with her family (including kitties Murr the Shy, Smush the Cuddlebucket, and Dimples the family extrovert) in Wilmington. She teaches in the Multimedia Communication Department at Wesley College in Dover, a commute which might be causing an addiction to audiobooks.

Between The Two
Burky Achilles

Mom asks about the bruise on my cheek. I am ten and know better than to look down the barrel of her twelve-gauge tongue. I tell her something believable—I got shoved around the school bus. Again. As she shakes her head, the little ringlets in front of each ear, the ones she so carefully pins each night, come uncoiled along with words shot straight from the heart of those red lips. What is the matter with you that you… If you were more outgoing… stood up straight… showed a little more interest… your appearance…

I stop listening, mesmerized by the spectacle of her coming undone—black hairs springing into small coils at her temples and forehead, pink blotches blooming on her cheeks, blue eyes backlit by some ferocity I cannot fathom. I know what is coming. If I behaved as her daughter, rather than my father's son, I would not be such an easy target.

The color picture is faded now. In it, I am little, freckled, maybe five. Dad is stripped to the waist. We are standing in the front yard of the pink house, the house we rented in 1962, our first year on Kauai. His jeans tell the tale of campfire and the sharp iron of dried blood, of stale beer and sweat, and of two days worth of machete work and hiking through valley underbrush tracking goat with our neighbor Dickey Silva. Dad's arms are scratched, his nails caked with dirt and browned blood. A broad smile hides small, square teeth.

The goat head between us is heavy. Flies cling where it was severed. I search his glassy eyes to see if dying hurt, but he is not saying. At five, my fingers cannot close all the way around the horn. In the late afternoon heat, my small hand slips along the bumpy ridges. My lips and eyes are pinched into squinty lines against the effort. Mom tells me to lift my side up just a little higher and smile. I try. Right before she snaps the Kodak, my arm and smile go slack from the weight of it.

That evening, Dad sits on the back steps in his boxers with his rifle and a beer. The first thing you do is make sure your gun is unloaded. He empties the last round from the chamber and holds it out to me. The bullet is gold with a hard tip and I try to imagine how the goat must have felt when it pierced him. This is the bolt, Dad says, thick index finger resting on the round knob. He slides it out and lays it across my upturned palms. The shaft is oily and heavy like a half-full sack of marbles. Dad sips his beer, checks over his shoulder to make sure Mom's out of sight and then offers me a sip. It tastes terrible.

Dad lays the gun across his lap, attaches the cleaning rod to the bore brush, dips it in solvent and pushes the brush through the bore all the way out the end. I crouch next to him and count as he pushes and pulls the brush through the bore in a steady rhythm. He takes me though each step—after the cleaning the oiling, after the oiling the reassembly. There is no hurry. And there is an order and reason to each step. This is pretty much how my dad showed me when I was your age, he says. Are you going to teach me to shoot someday? I ask. The smile in his eyes shifts a bit as if to make room for new thought.

The next day Mom has errands in Lihue. In the close air of the Chevy, her Jean Nate mingles with Final Net. She tames her thicket of her black hair into a sleek French roll. A perfect spiral curl in front of each ear frames her face. Her skin is unblemished and her red nails are flawless. On her lips is a matching shade that leaves a puckered kiss on the end of each cigarette filter in the blue glass ashtray. My chore is to empty and wipe out that ashtray each day before Dad gets home.

We are quiet in the car and the force of each turn pushes my body side to side. The only thing keeping me from sliding across the vinyl is the sweat on the back of my thighs. I want to say slow down. Instead, I dig my fingers into the armrest on the door. With Mom, it is usually best to just keep quiet and hang on.

Mom and I go to Kauai Stores—Mom's favorite. Rounders packed with blouses, skirts, slacks, and muumuus are a magnet. She is always on the hunt for something and today she rifles through blouse after blouse, rounder after rounder, stopping briefly to consider anything blue or the texture of certain silky fabrics. She is what the hippies call, in her groove.

Her rules: be quiet, do not slouch, do not wander. Look cute. After fifteen minutes, I feel my body begin to fold in on itself with boredom and my feet fall into their familiar rubber slipper shuffle. My wavy hair has shot the manacles of barrette and bobby pin. Red dirt smears my green gingham shorts.

I drift in Mom's wake. Run my hands through the blouses she has passed, smell the sizing clinging to all that new fabric. I slip through a curtain of blouses into the middle of the rounder almost by accident. From here I am completely hidden. By some miracle, Mom moves to an adjoining rounder without me. I am left to spy on other women, stare blatantly even, and hold my breath as they flick through the same blouses Mom has passed up, the material liquid, then stiff, then coarse across my skin in rapid fire. This is the most fun I have ever had shopping.

After what seems like a long time, I slide through the blouses and step into the glaring store light. Mom has moved on. In fact, after searching, it seems she has left the entire department. I try to find where we were, but through tears all the blouses and rounders look the same. A lady with a nametag that says, Leilani, leads me to the counter. The manager is called. He asks my name, age, where I live—the pink house. They page Mom over the PA system. She doesn't come, but a policeman does. As the minutes tick by, my panic blooms. By the time Officer Akana slides in next to me on the front seat of his cruiser, I can barely breathe.

At the station, Officer Akana offers me a leftover malasada and a Coke. My cheeks fill with sweet dough and sugar and grease. I realize how hungry I am. Hungry enough to stop crying and just eat, in that hard chair next to the secretary's desk. By the time Mom blows through the door, it is almost a surprise. Sleepy, I nearly dozed off. Her blue eyes burn. She apologizes to the secretary, to Officer Akana, and explain to anyone else who will listen to how I wandered off, how she searched, how she was outside, frantic, looking for me by the time they paged her.

The next day Mom asks if I am sorry. Sorry for what? Sorry I had to spend an entire afternoon lost in Kauai Stores rather than checking the gecko eggs about to hatch under the lychee tree? Sorry for her embarrassment or sorry that I am not girly enough with my flyaway hair and dirty green shorts? At five I don't know what to say, so I say yes.

One day when I am ten and trapped in the house vacuuming after school, I go over the parts of Dad's rifle in my mind—stock, trigger, lock, sight, barrel, bolt, chamber—like a mantra and my mind stumbles onto the horrifying fact that my being a girl is squeezing out my wild time. Bike racing the boys down the cane haul road behind our cul-de-sac, bass fishing in the reservoir and hunting for lillikoi and guava and star fruit to gorge on before dinner are being replaced, one by one, with girl chores.

Mom is an expert homemaker. As her daughter, it is taken for granted I will follow in her footsteps. From an early age I have helped indoors. At five, Mom gave me a miniature working iron and ironing board. I burned my fingers and managed to scorch several of Dad's hankies before she called it quits.

Each birthday brings additional chores with new instructions for exactly how, when and where to dust, vacuum, feed the dogs, make Jell-O, and now salad. The way each chore is done is as important as the result. Mom's way is the way and even at ten, I can see where this is all leading. The bigger I get, the smaller the house.

My heart constricts a little more with each hour spent indoors with the chores and Mom. Being shut in the house with her is like being locked in a burning building and waiting for rescue that never comes. I have tried to shift my allegiance and help Dad in the yard, but each time I try, he sends me back inside to Mom where the air is thick and confining. My wild time is shrinking.

A few months later, Dad rolls in early from work. I have nearly finished my chores and am sitting outside on the back stoop biding my time, waiting to feed the dogs. He tells me go ahead and feed them early. My eyes shift to the kitchen window. Mom is just inside at the sink. He hollers through the open screen that he needs me for a few errands and points to the truck.

We drive up to the foothills behind Wailua Falls, where he begins to teach me how to shoot an old .22 Winchester. He shows me how to brace straight the front leg of my shooting hand, plant the rifle stock snug up into my cheek fat under the bone, set the stock square in the hollow niche of my shoulder. He trains me to sight the targets—a series of beer cans filled with water and balanced on fence posts and tree stumps. Keep your eye on the target. Do not look down the barrel of the gun. That is Medusa.

The first squeeze of the trigger kicks the rifle back hard into my cheek. I miss, but from there on out, know what to expect. It is hard to sight the target without staring down the barrel of the gun. On consecutive shots, I blink. Miss. Lift my face from the stock as I pull the trigger. Miss. Shift the weight off my straight front leg. Miss. Each time the stock slams into me—a new bruise. Dad will not let me quit until I score a hit, and I would never think to ask because I am not a quitter. There is something in the blast of each explosion that makes me feel alive—that smell of oil as the gun barrel heats up and the impact of the recoil against my cheek.

The hit, when it comes, is a surprise. The beer can explodes, blowing a rainbow spray of shrapnel. My cheek feels as though I have been punched, but I want to keep shooting. Want this time to last forever, Dad's calm voice close to my ear, his thick hands steadying my shoulder against the rifle's recoil.

The next day Dad pulls me aside out of Mom's earshot, because she would kill him if she knew, and asks if I am sore. I say no, but the bruise on my cheek tells it different. I get a pat on the back, a nod—high praise. Someday he will teach me to hunt. I am sure of it. After all, why would he teach me to shoot, if he wasn't going to teach me to hunt?

Burky Achilles began a spontaneous eruption of poetry in January of 2014, following the deaths of a good friend, her mother, and mother-in-law in 2013. She also writes essays and creative non-fiction. Her essays have appeared in the *Chocolate for a Woman's Soul* Series. "'A'ā," her first published poem, appeared online in the summer 2014 issue of *VoiceCatcher*. In addition, Burky won first-place in the poetry category at the 2015 Tucson Festival of Books Literary Awards. She was raised on the south shore of Kauai and received her Masters in Writing in Fiction from Portland State University in 2002. She is currently teaching English as a Second Language for a year at Amnat Chaoren High School in Amnat Chaoren, Thailand.

Dad-isms
Denise Clemons

My father taught me to drive
on quiet roads and gentle hills
Accelerate into the curve

I learned the Lindy
hearing him say
Loosen your feet

Falling into the surf
I found I could swim
Breathe through your mouth

He took off the training wheels
and ran alongside me
Pretend you are flying

Watching them fold the flag
I considered my decisions
Choose to contribute or consume

This morning, behind the wheel
balanced between clutch and brake
Accelerate into the curve

Denise Clemons holds a BA in Biopsychology from Vassar College and an MA in Writing from Johns Hopkins University. She spent the first twenty years of her career as an executive in the technology industry before leaving the corporate world to devote her energies to the non-profit arena. She lives in Lewes, Delaware where she writes a weekly cooking column for the *Cape Gazette* newspaper. Denise's poetry has been published in journals, chapbooks, and anthologies.

Day of the Dead
Peg Alford Pursell

When I was a child, Day of the Dead meant sugar skulls, staying up past midnight, marigolds, burning copal, blazing votives. I didn't recognize any of the faces in the photographs on the altar. Now I have my own dead—and no sweet bread, hot wax, or tequila to lure them, no fancy *papel picado*.

The dead come anyway, in fragments, perforated memories. My grandmother wearing a man's fedora, a secret greeting card folded into her dress pocket. My grandfather, who burned *basura* in his basement fireplace sending obscene odors throughout the neighborhood, whose last act was to eat a bowl of strawberry ice cream in the middle of the night. The crush I smoked pot with behind the brick chimney in the attic of his parents' home, wrapped up with me in his sleeping bag. He confessed he had no plan for after graduation, and he laughed, and he never needed the plan. The stillborn girl who looked like a baby bird with bulging eyes curled in a nest under the acacia. The man I'd once thought was the one, who wasn't, and whom I couldn't live with once I understood that, who on a tear of amphetamines put a gun to his head.

The dead. I want a belly of bravery. I want to know the kindness sent out of the cage of the heart. An eye that never becomes insensate to the invisible spectrum, an ear that never dulls to the song of the pulse. The night grows long until it's short, and the sweetened tongue kisses the breath, and the breath is the breath is the breath.

Peg Alford Pursell is the author of the forthcoming book of stories, *Show Her a Flower, a Bird, a Shadow* (ELJ Publications). Her work has been published in or forthcoming from *Permafrost*, the *International Journal of Compressed Arts*, *RHINO*, the *Los Angeles Review*, among others, and shortlisted for the Flannery O'Connor Award. A graduate of the Warren Wilson MFA Program for Writers, she lives in the San Francisco Bay Area and curates Why There Are Words in Sausalito, a well-regarded literary reading series she founded five years ago.

Petal
Margaret Mizushima

The veins on my mama's hands stood out like earthworms on a sidewalk.

"Petal," she said, her voice thin and petulant with disease, "you come over t' here where I can see you."

"Yes, Mama."

"You're always lurkin' round the edge of the room like you're as ashamed as you should be."

"Ashamed?"

"Lookit you. All dressed up in your nursey clothes, still fat as a hog."

"Yes, ma'am."

"I told your daddy you'd never mount to nothing. What a waste of money the gov'ment spent on your schooling. Here you are, come back to prey on my good nature, eat me outta house and home."

"I came because you asked me to, Mama. To take care of you."

"Musta been out of my mind."

"Yes, ma'am."

"Don't you sass me, girlie. I may be dyin', but I'm not dumb."

"Yes, Mama."

A sly look consumed her face, and I saw her go inside herself, muttering the litany she'd started about a week ago. She ignored me now. "Gotta take care of Rosie. Gotta make sure Rosie knows she'll get it all."

"I called Rose for you, Mama. She said she's too busy to come."

"She's my pretty girl. Lookit her, county Spud Bowl Queen. All you did in high school was poke your nose in a book."

I'd always been larger than my older sister, but I'd felt lesser than. The Petal to her Rose.

"Did you call that lawyer fella?"

I crossed my fingers behind my back to cancel the lie. "He'll be by later today, Mama."

"Gotta get my affairs in order. Can't leave it to the state."

"Yes, Mama."

I drew a syringe full of Succinylcholine, a powerful paralytic I'd stolen from the hospital I'd left to come here. An overdose would cause shutdown of the respiratory system. "Time for your pain medicine, Mama."

"It's about time. You're a cold girl. I think you enjoy seein' me suffer."

"No, ma'am."

"My poor body looks like a pin cushion."

True. An array of colorful bruises mottled her hands. One more needle stick would never be noticed. I slipped the needle into a vein.

"This should take only a few minutes, Mama."

Seemed like she'd had it coming for a lifetime.

Margaret Mizushima is the author of *Killing Trail: A Timber Creek K-9 Mystery*, released December 8, 2015 by Crooked Lane Books. After earning a master's degree in speech pathology, Margaret practiced in a hospital and then in a multi-disciplinary rehab clinic that she owned and managed. After the sale of her company, she joined her husband in managing their veterinary clinic and Angus cattle herd. Her short story "Hay Hook" was published in the 2014 Rocky Mountain Fiction Writers anthology *Crossing Colfax*. She currently lives in Colorado on a small farm where she and her husband raised two daughters and a multitude of animals. She can be found on Facebook, on Twitter @margmizu, and on her website at www.margaretmizushima.com.

Love and Other Drugs
Melissa Jefferson

The record player played
non-stop that summer.
Spinning riffs of lazy saxophone
mirrored hot, drowsy days.
Seductive caramel voices filled
her space, drifted
out the door, down the street
sharing heartbreak, tailspin.

A constellation of stressors,
youth, fragility, duty...
a dose of,
Is that all there is?
preceded the saxophone summer.
Then, a collapse-
salvation
in the form of illness.

Her hysteria, her nervous breakdown,
her dis-ease,
was treated by a vacation to
the psych ward where
men in white, dutifully
restrained, sedated, and administered
complimentary shock therapy.

Lethargic
but resilient
she rested, and
spent the summer reorganizing
her record collection,
reconstructing her life
song by song.

Melissa Jefferson has been an exporter, copywriter, facilitator of parent and teen skills classes, a lifelong horse woman, and an equine assisted learning services professional. She returned to university in 2009, and graduated from Colorado Mesa University in 2013 with a BA in Psychology. A class in Creative Writing and a Women Writing for a Change program kindled Melissa's desire to write.

In 2015, Melissa and her partner developed, wrote, and self-published, *Horsepower for Survivors – Equine Assisted Group Therapy Curriculum for Sexually Abused Children*.

She is a 4th generation Coloradoan and lives on a dirt road in Western Colorado where she and her husband peacefully coexist with two dogs, several hives of honeybees, and too many horses.

Phoenix

Thea Williams

The funeral was on a Saturday, wet and cold, as if the heavens themselves couldn't accept what had happened. The family, though divided by divorce and distance, banded together as one. The father, blindingly handsome, carried himself with dignity, supporting his erstwhile wife in every phase of the proceedings. The remaining son, just graduated from college, tried valiantly to accept his new responsibility as sole heir.

But the mother carried the day.

After an interminable service fraught with needless delays during which the bereaved family found themselves on display as if this were a freak show, the elegant, black-clad woman took the podium. With the boy's father standing behind her and at times bracing her with his hands, she delivered her message.

"If you have the addictive gene, you can be sure you'll become an addict. My son, when he was playing baseball as a child, didn't aspire to this. He fought viciously against it, but in the end, seeking the high took him higher than he could have ever imagined."

Here she paused and pointed heavenward, and everyone knew she didn't mean the domed ceiling of the magnificent church.

"Learn from this!" she pleaded. "Don't let my son's death be in vain! Let the Lord be your high! And, for God's sake, if you have an addiction problem, get help..."

Her strong, steady voice trailed off into the unspoken. Everyone in the audience silently filled in the end of her sentence: "So that your families don't have to go through what we're going through."

The remaining son and his fellow pallbearers, most of whom barely filled out the dark suits they had probably bought for the occasion, joined the procession to perform their final act of kindness for the deceased. The parents, whose marriage had come apart, came together one last time to escort their firstborn to his last journey.

When the sorrowful party arrived outside the church, they found that the slow, steady rain had become a drenching downpour. Umbrellas were opened, hearse and limos loaded.

The guest made her way to her car. She reflected on her newly graduated son, who had called during the service. She had almost let the call go to voice mail, but followed a gut impulse to whisper into the phone despite the grieving going on around her.

Some instinct inside knew she must attend to the living even amidst the dead.

Being reminded where his mother was, the young man on the phone apologized for interrupting, and simply asked if the dishes in the dishwasher were clean so he could put them away. At that point, the guest's eyes, which had remained surprisingly dry throughout the service, felt tears come to them.

The guest had two strong impulses on her way home. One was to make a meal, to create something which would be of value, something life-giving.

The other was to make a call.

"Hello?" an expectant young voice chirped on the other end of the line.

When the guest identified herself, her niece laughed and said she knew who it was. Whether it was caller ID or the sound of the older woman's voice that gave her away didn't matter; the aching mourner just felt happy to be recognized and warmly welcomed by one who had been a stranger not long ago.

Clearing her throat, the guest stated the reason for her call.

"I just came from a funeral of a young man who OD'd," she began, "and I just had to call and thank you for choosing sobriety. I know it's one day at a time, but, just, thanks."

The younger woman responded sweetly, as her aunt had known she would. A few short years ago, drugs had put distance and difficulty into all the young girl's relationships. Now, she had forged strong bonds within her family and community. The aunt no longer feared and distrusted her niece. She told the girl she was one of her favorite people, and they both knew she meant it.

"By the way," the recovering addict remarked as if discussing the weather, "Don't mention this to anyone, 'cause they'll all make a big deal and wanna have a party or something, but I have four years of sobriety today."

The aunt hugged her verbally and felt more tears fall.

Then she went home to her son and made a meal.

At age 52, Thea Williams is a beginner in the writing profession, but has had several articles published in *Focus on the Family Magazine* and Al Anon's *The Rap*. She also writes a blog *Morsels for Meditation* at reflectionsbythea.blogspot.com.

An alumnus of Villanova University ('89, Summa Cum Laude, BA, Liberal Arts and Sciences), Thea serves as paraprofessional for Haverford School District, as well as private home health aide. A divorced mother of two adult sons, she lives in Havertown, PA and enjoys vacationing along the East Coast. One of the highlights of Thea's life was visiting the New England homes of her childhood inspiration, Louisa May Alcott.

He Doesn't Have to Say Anything
Caroline Block

He doesn't have to say anything to wake you. You had already taken to not sleeping. He paces the length of your bed, two steps and back. He's left twenty dollars for emergencies in his top dresser drawer. You have to understand. He'll be back on Sunday or Monday. He has to go.

You are twelve. You can understand—but you are dumb, wide-eyed, knowing only that mothers and fathers leave even when they say don't want to go.

His breath, full of coffee, fires down on you. His freshly laundered shirt, full of starch, is one of the last ones Millie pressed. You had promised him that you'd learn to iron. He said that he didn't mind wrinkles.

A wave of rubbing alcohol shoots from him. Scraps of toilet paper stick to his face like flies. His shirt is tucked into his pants. His belt is cinched. His black curly hair is sheared for summer. The crew cut shows off his dimples, hairy ears, sunburned neck, his manliness and boyishness. He is gangly, restless, careful not to lean against your legs or arms or hips as he bends over you. Long ago he stopped claiming your hand when crossing streets; he hasn't touched you, not a kiss, not anything in ever so long. This past week, he couldn't even hold your gaze.

His hand hovers over your head. You freeze. He must be thinking that you are asleep with your eyes open. He did remark last week that you are growing like a weed, that you are looking more like your mother, even as you raced to the bathroom and searched the mirror for clues. When he turned away, you didn't follow him. You didn't want him to think that you were afraid of the responsibility of remembrance.

Now in the dark, you kick off your sheet.

"Toots," he says. "Tell your brothers and sister not to worry." He is going to find his heart's desire, and return to all of you, a happy man, and even though he says none of this, you can make yourself believe it.

You can smell the harsh soap on his palms and you hold your breath tight.

"I got to go," he says, pulling away.

He crosses to Jennifer's bed. She stirs. She sucks her thumb surrounded by dolls. Some are missing arms or legs, one is headless, dismembered in your efforts to fix her, or so you told your younger sister. They dolls are tucked alongside her at night. He knows better than to touch her. If she wakes, she'll squeeze her arms around his neck, wrestle him to her, flay against his chest, and plead for him to take her and the dolls too. He flees.

The hardwood floors echo his steps until, as you strain to listen, he is next door in your brothers' room. Matthew's hoarse snores penetrate the walls.

He is one year younger and more than three and a quarter inches shorter than you. If he were a shape, it would be square. He has black rings under his eyes and a perpetually runny nose. He likes to draw, and papers and sharp pencils will be skewed around his bed like armaments. Your father always says that Matthew needs to toughen up. If your father takes one of you, he'll take Matthew, but Matthew will not last long. He'll run away, and you will never see Matthew again. You will miss Matthew.

Or, he may take Gabriel with him, the only blond among all of you, a strange creature, bone-thin with burnt brown summer skin as if he spent his days rolling in the dirt. Your father can easily carry Gabriel into the car, can drive away with him, and Gabriel will sleep on. And when Gabriel wakes, he will be happy. He will agree to do anything, go anywhere, in return for attention to his lost cause of being the youngest, forever the one your father squints at as if recalling an acquaintance whose name he forgot.

You press your ear against the wall. Your father might change his mind and stay. You should be used to him saying one thing and doing another.

The front door— then the screen door— opens and slams.

You won't rise until he returns. A breeze shudders across your bedroom. The wood-framed windows pucker, all pushed up, swollen with humidity. The summer resides as much inside the house as outside: whirring with mosquitoes and crickets, lush with overgrown hedges and trees scraping up to the second floor, empty now. Until last week, Millie lived upstairs from Monday through Friday. Last Sunday night, at the time when he would usually go to the train station to retrieve Millie, he pointed out a cardinal flitting from tree to tree in the backyard and swore when it flew away. He cursed that he couldn't watch any more news. That he was wasting his life watching the news. That it was time to turn off the damn idiot box, but he didn't turn it off, the light flickering in the twilight.

"We have to go get Millie," you reminded him.

"I had to let her go."

"Let her go where?"

He flung the Sunday newspapers next to his chair, scattering the print, the news in disarray.

"What about Millie, when is she coming back?"

"She's not."

"She said she loved us," I said, and then added, "Would you ever leave us?"

"No." He stormed out of the house with a bag of birdseed in the crook of his arm like a fat baby. On the front lawn, he side armed the seed out into the uncut grass.

You wanted to tell him that you were old enough to take care of the house and your brothers and sister, and him, too.

You just wished he had warned you. You would have said good-bye to her, and in response, Millie would have wrapped her arms around you. She'd have pushed you into her breasts, near her heart, with a honey, honey, honey. You could drown in that heart.

*   *   *   *   *

You bury your face in your pillow, open your mouth, loosen your tongue. But it's no good kissing the pillow, no good pretending it's some boy this morning.

Once you waited for your mother alone like this. She had promised you that she would take you to the pool after your nap. But you didn't nap; you changed into your polka dot bathing suit, your favorite at six-years-old and waited for her. When you heard her rustling, you rose after her, not one for sleeping even then. She had taken to wearing a sweater all the time, and she had on her white one, with wool so soft, you loved to stroke her in it. She said she was only scooting outside to have a word or two with Uncle Stanley. You could see his motorcycle from your bedroom window: the silver chrome and his blond head with the shoulder-length hair bobbing to music. He wasn't your real uncle. Don't open the door for anyone. I will be home before you are all done with your nap. When she kissed your head, her perfume was left in your hair. You could smell it for days. Later, your father returned home from work, and you had been alone for hours with your siblings. In the basinet, Gabriel stirred inside his wrappings. You had even given him a bottle, one of those that your mother had prepared for him, and you were still in your bathing suit as were Matthew and Jennifer. Your father said you had to be a big girl. You had to sit still now and listen: Your mother was dead. Killed in a motorcycle accident.

"With Uncle Stanley?"

"Sure. Keep calling him that."

*   *   *   *   *

Your father's battered minivan smoked out of the driveway, and you raced down the hall, past his unmade bed, passed the baskets of dirty laundry, and flung open the front door, stretching out your hands as if to pull him back inside.

"Don't go." Your first words of the day were too little, too late.

The minivan sped up at the Smyth's next door, who were getting divorced.

When Mr. Smyth had moved out of his house it was with a big show of satchels and pressed dress shirts hung from dark to light on a pole across the back of his BMW. And you think now: That is how you leave forever—with all the shirts you own.

Her father would return. Sunday or Monday, or when he could.

Yesterday, Mrs. Smyth had charged at him as soon as he pulled the minivan into the driveway. "Your daughter destroyed my American beauties, Martin."

"I'm sure we don't have any roses in the house, do we?" he asked you.

"Please, the truth. I have had enough lies," Mrs. Smyth said with a fierce little laugh, seeking out your father through her thick glasses. "And you," she said, not even glancing in your direction near the deflowered plants. "Let's stand up straight, please. I will always believe in proper posture."

All those roses—all the pinks and reds and whites—you had plucked them all apart. Those petals— you had waved them over your lips, rubbed them into your cheeks, the rose-smell penetrating you. You had fluttered the petals up and down your bare arms and up and down Jennifer and Gabriel's arms, and then at his insistence, Matthew's too. You could have buried yourself in those petals from all those roses. "We don't have any American beauties in our house," you said, but neither seemed to hear you.

* * * * *

At the end of the block, the headlights of the minivan jolt into the bend, flashing like searchlights.

Don't go.

And the lights disappear.

And you spin around.

You've never been outside this early. As the world whirls—the wind picks up, the evergreen, the tallest one, snaps forward, birds riddle out, and Johnny Smyth drives his sky blue Camaro toward his house and eases it into his driveway. He whistles out the window at you like he's trying to be funny.

"Sure thinks he's something," your father said last week, watching Johnny slide into the Camaro. "But then didn't we all once believe the sun rose just for us?"

You think of all the boys you liked to pretend-kiss and how you never dared to include Johnny. Yet this morning, you stop and whistle back, a short, dry-mouth imitation. Your white cotton nightgown billows out. Your bare feet play with pebbles from the cracks in the driveway.

His eyes are red-rimmed, and he slouches against the side of his car.

"I can see right through whatever you're wearing," he says.

You wait for him to say more—he hasn't said this much to you in years—but he only dips his head away from your waiting gaze. "I'm going to sleep," he says. "And so should you."

He slips inside his house.

Your nightgown shimmies up your legs, which are riddled with mosquito bites. You scratch. You shake you hair out—you have a rat's nest in there according to Millie who had spent way too much time trying to brush it out, going honey, honey, honey, stand still, as she tugged the hairbrush through the knots.

You jump up and down. Your father always says that you have ants in your pants—that he got you economy-size on account of your height—that you are probably somebody else's daughter—and you realize that you are remembering this as if it happened a long time ago and not in the past week.

A pair of cardinals appears right before you and peck at the stray birdseed, distracting you. You consider that you should return to your bedroom, to your bed, to the yield of your pillow. Your arms stretch out, your skin prickles in the cool air. You hop from one foot to another. You wait for the road to rise and reverse itself, for the mini-van to re-emerge and return. The sun lays ribbons across the horizon. You don't hear the front door re-open, or the steps behind you.

"You know I can see your driveway from my bedroom window." Next to you, Johnny has changed into gym shorts and a tee shirt, the cross scents of fields and lockers. You think he has come out to exercise, for an early morning run.

He doesn't wait for you to answer that you had taken to not sleeping, that you remember best in the early morning. He's not here to hear that your father will be home soon—Sunday or Monday, or when he can. Johnny hangs his sweatshirt with its high school letters for track and baseball around your shoulders and looks down toward the end of the block too.

"I couldn't sleep either," he says.

He doesn't have to say anything else.

* * * * *

You are old now and you sleep even less. You rise, and your father, long dead, leaves you every dawn.

Caroline Bock is the author of two critically acclaimed young adult novels: *Lie* (St. Martin's Press, 2011) and *Before My Eyes* (St. Martin's Press, 2014). Her short stories and poetry have been published or are forthcoming in *Akashic Press*, *Gargoyle Magazine* and its *Defying Gravity Anthology*, *Fiction Southeast*, *100 Word Story*, *Ploughshares*, *Prometheus*, *Vestal Review*, and *Zero Dark-Thirty*. Caroline is a graduate of Syracuse University, where she studied creative writing with Raymond Carver. As of 2011, she holds a MFA in fiction from The City College of New York, where received the school's top prize in writing for children's literature. Prior to focusing on her writing, she led for many years the marketing and public relations departments at Bravo cable network, IFC and IFC Films. She is 52 years old and lives in Maryland with her husband and two children.

Beyond Niagara
Maria Keane

We view elegance
from a safe distance,

feel the hard earth,
straddle the wire walk.

A cradle of spume
births glacial mist,

melts ice, carves
a pounding on the rocks.

Wear your blue poncho—
disconsolate you.

Your silence roars
in the cavern of my mind.

Footsteps move with caution on
stones, warning of a crystalline path.

Slivers of speech persist:
nettled conversation begs forgiveness.

Maria Keane served as adjunct Professor of Fine Arts at Wilmington University, New Castle Delaware from 1984-2009. She received her MA from the University of Delaware (Phi Kappa Phi.) Maria, a visual artist and a published poet, is an Arts and Letters member of the National League of American Pen Women, the Howard Pyle Studio of Wilmington and the National Association of Women Artists. The Philadelphia Writers' Conference, and the National League of American Pen Women has awarded her poetry. Maria has contributed ekphrastic poems to the Biggs Museum of American Art from 2005-2011. She was awarded a Professional Fellowship jointly from the NEA and the Delaware Division of the Arts in 1997.

The Getaway
Andrea Jarrell

Susannah was murdered just before Christmas. I didn't hear the terrible news until after New Year's, when a friend called me on my way home from a family holiday out of town. The house where she'd been killed was just a hundred yards or so from ours, poking up from behind trees across the road. Nothing between us except our long driveway and adjacent pond. Not that I could have stopped what had happened, even if we'd been home. We probably would have been sitting in our living room watching TV or upstairs reading bedtime stories to our two kids. We probably wouldn't even have heard the gunshots.

When it happened, the co-op preschool that her son and my son and daughter attended was already on the holiday break. My husband Brad and I had loaded up our SUV, bundled the kids into their car seats, and driven down to Portland—Maine, not Oregon. From there we'd flown to Michigan, to my in-laws' house with its big Christmas tree and glittering ornaments. In the days before Facebook and Twitter, we'd remained blissfully cocooned and cut off from the rest of the world.

I didn't understand at first why I reacted to the news of Susannah's death the way that I did. Yes, there was the shocking violence of it. And the throat-catching sadness for her little boy, and the wrongness of anyone snatched from life, much less someone so young. But there was more to it than that. Especially when I admitted to myself that I hadn't actually liked Susannah. Or, more accurately, I hadn't allowed myself to like her.

The truth is, I'd always been a little afraid of her. After she was killed, I understood why.

Brad and I had been in Maine for a few years by then. In our early thirties, we were just starting out in our marriage and our life as parents. We'd always been city people before. Our move from Los Angeles to the idyllic town of Camden was the first of what we expected would be many adventures in our life together. Camden is the childhood home of Edna St. Vincent Millay, the town where the movie *Peyton Place* was filmed, and, rumor has it, a haven for retired CIA spies. Locals looking to move know to put their houses on the market during the summer, when tourists fall in love with the quaintness of it all: the harbor, the lupine-covered hills, the age-old stone walls, the black and white Oreo cows. But Maine winters are for a hardy few, and the smart lookey-loos come to their senses before any money changes hands.

We moved to Camden knowing what we were getting into. Brad had been offered a two-year gig at the Institute for Global Ethics, to work on a project about running positive political campaigns. I saw the move as a way to leave my workaday life as the PR director of a small college—to trade in my pantyhose and suits for jeans and sweaters and get back to writing. Fully expecting to return to L.A. in a couple of years, we found tenants for our small house. But the two-year project turned into two more, and five years after moving we finally unloaded the L.A. house, unsure if we would ever head west again.

Moving to Camden felt a little like we'd entered the witness protection program—so far from everyone we'd known, plunked down into a new life. I took to that life more easily than one might expect, embracing it with "pinch me" elation: pancakes on Sundays, a fully-stocked pantry with an extra freezer for meat, trips to the pumpkin patch, red wagons in the driveway, rain boots and slickers, mittens and parkas. This was the stuff of ordinary families, which I'd carefully observed during childhood sleepovers. Having grown up in small apartments with my single mother, who was much more interested in books and travel than picket fences and seasonal door wreathes, I kept waiting for the residents of Camden to discover that I didn't belong.

Oh, I knew how to look the part at Mommy and Me music classes, or when it was my turn to handle a baking project at the preschool, or while hanging out under a wide- brimmed straw hat at the local beach, my kids appropriately slathered with sunscreen and playing with sand pails and shovels. But I still felt inferior, the way I had as a kid when I would tell friends and their parents that my mother was a lawyer rather than a legal secretary. I told that lie right up through college, even though the thought of being found out made me queasy.

Certain people hatched such lies in me—in Camden, people like Kim Tate and her husband Jack. Kim was a tall, athletic blond who'd gone to Yale. She'd met Jack—also tall, but dark and handsome enough—on the train between New Haven and New York City one afternoon when they were both in college. With their good looks and money, the Tates were small-town famous. Other mothers at our preschool had a crush on Jack, one of them going so far as to tell Kim that she looked forward to receiving their photo Christmas card so she could moon over him. I had more of a crush on Kim, whose three perfect little children were spaced a year and a half apart, lined up like cherub-faced Russian dolls in hand-knitted sweaters she'd designed and made.

Our oldest kids—Kim's and mine—were in the fours and fives class at the co-op preschool along with Susannah's son. If Kim was on the elite end of the social spectrum, Susannah was on the other. Or at least that's where—I admit now—I put her. Almost from the moment I met her, something about Susannah made me steer clear. When I saw her faded, rust-colored Toyota in the school's parking lot, I stayed in my own car, behind darkened windows. I waited to go inside until after she and her son emerged from the school—their fingers laced, the day's artwork flapping in Susannah's other hand.

She was one of those pretty girl-women—twenty-one, twenty-three, twenty-five? If she hadn't been a mother, she might have seemed even younger, like a teenager with her whole life before her. I'd seen fathers at the preschool watching her, trying to be nonchalant as they homed in on her. You could tell that she'd grown up attracting such attention and was no longer surprised or moved by it. At first, I wondered if my impulse to avoid her was simple jealousy because she was younger and sexier than I was. Her short skirts and angled beret over long corn-silk hair displayed a confidence that I'd never had. Then I noticed that she avoided me and the other parents as well—never lingering to chat on the playground.

She smiled but hurried purposefully, gathering her son's lunchbox, backpack, and coat. My mother had projected a similar defensive smile when she attended school events or collected me from a sleepover. *Just we two*, she used to say. It dawned on me then that Susannah's confidence, like my mother's, was designed to let other parents know she was doing fine, even though we outnumbered her two to one. I could feel how tightly Susannah's hand grasped her son's as they exited the preschool, holding on to each other and their place in the world.

The only time that I can remember even talking to her was at my daughter's birthday party. It was July; all the preschool parents stood around on our wide green lawn as kids took turns barreling down the giant yellow Slip 'n Slide my husband had set up.

I happened to be standing next to Susannah when the gifts were opened. Her son's present was a wooden fairy wand that his mother had painted dark blue and topped with a glitter-encrusted star. She'd written my daughter's name in silver along the handle. We watched as my daughter opened the gift and ran her small hand along the scrolling letters of her name. Susannah leaned sideways to me, our shoulders touching, and said, "I knew she would like it. She's such an artist." I imagined them together in the co-op preschool on one of Susannah's days to help. I could see her asking my daughter about the painting she was working on. Susannah would've bent down to be eye-level, pushing her long blond hair behind one shoulder as she did.

Then one day, as I pulled into the preschool lot, I noticed a man sitting in the passenger seat of Susannah's car. He was my own neighbor—a fit, tanned man named Craig. He operated a moving, refuse, and antiques busi-

ness out of his home and adjacent barn. When we first arrived from Cali-
fornia, my husband had hired him to help move us in. Admiring his Yankee
entrepreneurism, my husband marveled, "He's got it covered. He'll move it,
dump it, or sell it."

I remember being inordinately happy to see my neighbor in Susannah's
car, happier still when I passed her familiar Toyota parked in front of his
house. It intrigued me to think of how they might have met. Perhaps he
had hired her to answer the phones for his business. Or they'd struck up a
conversation in Cappy's bar on Main Street. There was no question of why
Susannah would appeal to him. But I could also see why he would appeal
to her. In his late forties, he was attractive in a town where single men were
few and far between. She might have said to herself, *try older, try wiser.* He
would be a good provider, a role model for her little boy. I pictured them
together—sheets rumpled, his tanned workman's hands on her milky skin.
I imagined him thanking his lucky stars each day to have such a lovely girl
on his arm.

I'd once imagined such meetings for my mother: a new client or lawyer in
her firm, who would appear one day and change our lives. I wondered what
Susannah's secret was. How had she managed to find a partner and step into
a new, safer life when my mother had not?

* * * * *

Kim Tate was the one who caught me on my cell as my family and I drove
home from the airport. "I didn't know you two were close," she said. "I'm so
sorry," she kept saying as I sobbed after hearing the news. Sobbing that I
didn't understand at first because, of course, we were not close at all.

In my mind's eye, I could see Susannah sitting in my kitchen, drinking
coffee with me. I imagined her son playing with my kids on the floor of
our living room, but that had never happened. I hadn't wanted them at our
house. As cute as her son was, I'd written him off as damaged goods. Damaged the way I'd been at his age. Jealous of what my friends had, prone to
elaborate lies and petty thefts, hitting and hair pulling when no one was
looking.

It hadn't been Susannah's youth or prettiness that made me steer clear of
her and her son. It had always been their aloneness and my fear that if I got
too close, that old familiar "just we two," aloneness might rub off on me.

Like a bedtime story, my mother used to tell me of our escape into the
world from my father. She'd light a cigarette, press it to her elegant lips,
exhale, and begin. Benign stories at first. Later, the stories about his ve-

nereal disease and his cheating and her black eyes. But even in her early, seemingly innocent stories, there was always a little violence. Singeing her eyelashes and eyebrows trying to light the stove in their first apartment. My father breaking his arm in an arm-wrestle on his birthday—the bone splitting right through the camel hair jacket she'd given him. "His muscles were stronger than bone," she'd said with a trace of true awe.

Our neighbor Craig was a mild man, nothing like my father. And yet he'd acted on the same jealousy and possessiveness that my mother had run away from. My mother had also been a girl-woman. At nineteen, the day she first felt me move inside her was the day she began plotting how to leave my father. Scared of what this man who slept beside her with a gun under his pillow might do to us one day when my crying got too much for him or when yet another man admired her beauty. Somehow I'd given her the courage.

Was it her little boy Susannah was thinking of when she told Craig it was over? It wasn't hard to imagine Craig's desperate pleading as he tried to make her stay. My mother told me that my father did the same, how he threatened to commit suicide if she ever left him. I could picture Craig grabbing Susannah's arm. She would have tried to shake him off, her blond hair flying as she tossed the few things she'd brought to his house into an overnight bag. She would not have known that he'd gone to the barn to look for a gun.

My mother's getaway car had been a teal blue Corvair. She'd literally and figuratively strapped me in beside her from then on—her precious cargo. How I wished Susannah had just gotten in that rust-colored Toyota and driven as far away from Craig as possible. How I wanted to run to her now and wrap my arms around her.

He shot her twice, using an antique pistol from his shop. According to the papers, after he killed her, he called his grown son and left a message on the son's answering machine. "I've done something stupid," he said. Then he hung up and killed himself.

As my family and I drove down our road, past Craig's quiet house, I remembered the last time I'd seen Susannah's car in his driveway. The sense of relief I'd had, thinking she'd found her happy ending. Thinking she could loosen the grip on her small son's hand just a little because they were safe at last.

Passing our pond—frozen and covered in snow—I heard the car's engine labor as it climbed our long driveway and saw the ice crystalized on branches of barren trees. How I wanted to rewind the film and change Susannah's ending the way my mother had changed ours.

As we pulled into the garage, firewood neatly stacked and dry by the mudroom door, I told Brad I'd help him unload the suitcases in a minute. My fingers were already tapping out my mother's telephone number. I waited, still in my coat in the car, pressing my phone to my ear, listening for her voice, waiting for us to talk, just we two.

Andrea Jarrell's personal essays have appeared in *The New York Times* "Modern Love" column; *Narrative Magazine*; *Brain, Child*; *Full Grown People*; *Memoir Journal*; *Literary Mama*; *The Washington Post*; *Washingtonian Magazine*; *The Huffington Post*; and the award-winning anthology *My Other Ex: Women's True Stories of Leaving and Losing Friendships*, among other publications. She is a graduate of the Bennington College MFA program and the recipient of a Martin Dibner Emerging Writers Fellowship. Her forthcoming memoir will be published by Booktrope.

The Glass Eye
Suzanne Samuels

She had a glass eye from a beating she had taken when her husband lost his job at the foundry. Who could blame him, really? He couldn't have known that the punch would land so precisely or that his pinky ring would be so ruinous.

By the time her neighbor took her to the hospital, the eye had begun to ooze green. When she awoke from having the eye removed, she thought the sparks were from the anesthesia. Halos around fluorescent lights – like the corona around the sun, but more alive, as if viewed through a telescope.

When she finally looked in the mirror, she realized that the sparks were there, embedded in the iris of her glass eye. The doctor had tried to match the color of her remaining eye, but this new eye and its sparks were a vivid green – like the Emerald City of Oz.

She was more entranced by those sparks each time she looked in the mirror. And as the beatings intensified, the sparks became luminous, alive, even if she was not. Eventually, she closed her other eye so she couldn't see the squalor of that apartment or the bruises that spread on her arms and legs. She couldn't see the pity of her neighbors or the shame of her children. In time, the only real part of her was that glass eye. The rest was unreal, like the half-rememberings of a distant dream.

For many years, Suzanne Samuels was a professor of Political Science. She published three books and a number of articles in the field of law and politics. Recently, she left her position to devote her time to writing on a full time basis. Since making this career change, She has written a number of essays and short stories, and is currently at work revising her historical novel, *The Orphans' Wheel*. In 2015, she participated in the Yale Writers' Conference and looks forward to continue working to hone her writing.

Freefall
Alison Condie Jaenicke

"We're in a freefall into future. We don't know where we're going. Things are changing so fast, and always when you're going through a long tunnel, anxiety comes along. And all you have to do to transform your hell into a paradise is to turn your fall into a voluntary act. It's a very interesting shift of perspective and that's all it is... joyful participation in the sorrows and everything changes."
--Joseph Campbell, Sukhavati

I. Independence Day

At dusk, atop the parking deck, we wait for darkness to ascend, the sky to explode. Teenagers buzz—our kids, theirs—hanging out of hatchbacks, lazy, wondering aloud what time it will start. Nine-fifteen? Nine-thirty? We cannot say. Midyear days are languorously long. We gaze over the valley. Maggie leans her chin on the wall, ready for entrancement. Radios crackle, preparing to crank out tunes chosen to match the fireworks' dance. A few low explosions erupt, rattling like machine-guns, and everyone cheers, attends.

Throughout the show, Eli chatters. He explains how triangulation can help him figure the height of the bursts, why the still-low moon rises orange over Mount Nittany and how it will clear to white as it ascends. He wonders whether a song is the 1812 Overture and why so many fireworks are green and red (not red, white and blue). He blabbers about which songs he hates and why this is all so boring. His stream of words aggravates—hush, let us enjoy, I say—and yet they also inflame my love and admiration for him.

On either side of me, my children's shoulders nudge mine, warm, and I am basking in happy. Ahead, on the sky's dark canvas, hot sparks arrange themselves, flicker, crackle, drift to earth—silver streaks, pink puffs, flowers, anemones, jellies—here then gone.

Over the edge of the concrete wall, four stories below, small people pass on the asphalt. Suddenly, out of nothing, my mind spins out an image of my child falling to the road below (only one of them, which one I cannot determine, and it's too brutal to choose). My hands flutter over the edge, fragile as butterfly wings. They can do nothing: the descent is irreversible. The violence of the thump brings me to my knees to vomit. I see my life halted.

A mother's milk dries up and yet she is still a mother. A child's life is truncated, and yet the mother feels that life still, a phantom limb that still itches, hurts, longs to move.

II. Tightrope

We knew a man who moved from one house to another on our street. First, he was the man who lived on a corner lot where he stretched a cable from one tall pine tree to another, forming a triangle. In the center of the tightrope, he secured a bicycle and posed a male mannequin atop it, jaunty cap and sunglasses on his head, a hand raised to wave to passersby. When the man moved to a house up the street, closer to us, the mannequin came down and did not seem to move with him. His new house was a plain box with a crumbling brick retaining wall wiggling between him and his neighbor. From chatting at the bus stop and from waving to his mannequin, we knew him slightly. We did not know that he was a skydiver, had completed more than 70 dives in the past three years, and worked a second job for Skydive Happy Valley, keeping their website and filing jumpers' paperwork.

On Saturday, July 7, at around 10 a.m., this neighbor, 53-year-old Chris Brown, stepped out of an airplane and plunged 4,000 feet. When balled up, a skydiver has a terminal velocity of about 200 miles per hour; with arms and feet fully extended to catch the wind, he slows to about 125 miles per hour. On this day, Chris' main chute opened but tangled, and his emergency chute failed; he spiraled to the ground and to his death.

A few weeks after he died, Chris' grown kids—even those who had never jumped before—parachuted in his memory, a memorial jump that involved 35 seconds of free fall and a five-minute parachute ride to the ground. I try to imagine what drove them: a desire for disorientation, for moving sideways with the plane while looking down toward their drop; a yearning for dizzy, exhilarating fear to intoxicate their blood, chemically bonding them to their dad; a need for wind to rush against their skin in such a way that the indelible ink of his death would erase or at least fade.

Reading about our neighbor's fall from the sky returned me to the previous week's image from the parking deck. Dreaming, waking, those three long seconds came to me—one-Mississippi, two-Mississippi, three-Mississippi—seconds in which I would know while my child was in the air that I could not affect the outcome. That he or she saw the ground coming, knew what came next, and could do nothing. (Repeatedly, like a heartbeat, the words: Did Chris know? Did others see him and know?) My reaction played and replayed in my head: I drop to my knees and pull out my innards like a magician pulling out silk scarves. I pull and pull until all that is inside has come out. Until down is up. Until fireworks stream from ground to sky, film reel in reverse. Rewind.

III. Descent without Drogue

When traditional skydiving becomes humdrum, one can move on to BASE jumping—parachuting from a fixed object or landform. BASE stands for the four categories of fixed objects from which one can jump: buildings, antennas, spans (bridges), and earth (cliffs).

By the 1990s, after years of skydiving, Austrian skydiver and stuntman Felix Baumgartner decided to "extend his canopy skills" with BASE jumping. His many daring and record-breaking jumps around the world include the following. In 2003, he became the first to cross the English Channel in freefall by crossing from Dover to Calais. In 2004, he set a world record for a BASE jump from the highest bridge in the world, Millau Bridge, France (1,125 feet). In 2007, he jumped into the second biggest cave in the world, called "Seating of the Spirits," in Oman (396 feet) and jumped off the world's tallest building, 101 Tower, Taipei (1,669.95 feet).

In the fall of 2012, the world watched and waited as Baumgartner prepared to float to what was billed "the edge of space" on his drop back to earth. After a few false starts when weather and winds scrapped the mission, on the morning of October 14, 2012, 65 years to the day that Chuck Yeager broke the sound barrier in an airplane, Baumgarter tethered himself to a helium-inflated balloon and rose nearly 24 miles above New Mexico. Beneath this huge upside-down teardrop, his capsule dangled like a silver bauble. At 128,100 feet, he opened the hatch. Far beneath him lay a glowing shield, blue and curved. In his white man-on-the-moon suit, face hidden behind smoked helmet window, he stood at the threshold, teetering, the capsule a silver turtle shell on his back. Breathing erratic and loud, rasping through the receiver, he managed a few words: "Sometimes you have to go up really high to understand how small you are. I'm going home now."

And then he stepped off the edge, willingly dropped into 4 minutes and 22 seconds of freefall, his body spinning near unconsciousness. For 35 seconds, he fought to control a "death spin." Later, "Fearless Felix" said, "It was much more difficult than many of us expected. In that situation, when you spin around, it's like hell and you don't know if you can get out of that spin or not." But he did. As he fell, the earth rose beneath him, everything blue at first, then warming to red then brown, the world finally separating again into familiar earth and sky.

In all, the trip back to earth lasted just over nine minutes. At his peak speed, he fell at 844 miles an hour, or Mach 1.25. He did it without "drogue," the extra parachute sometimes used to produce drag to slow down man or machine, to control and stabilize. His parachute floated him near the earth, and then, as if he'd simply jumped from a tree limb, he was running on solid ground, then kneeling, then talking about how humbling it was, this effort to travel to the edge of space, then turn around and surpass the speed of sound, hurtle toward home at more than 800 miles per hour and stand here with us, mortal once again.

IV. Not Plummeting, but Ascending

Why does one choose freefall? That feeling when the bottom drops out, all support gone, that weightlessness of organs, that fear that you will never stand safely on firm ground again. Across the nation, we line up for rides like the Drop of Doom, the Wild Eagle, the Stratosphere Tower's X Scream. We ski jump, bungee jump, hang-glide. Some of us yearn for the fear inherent in dangerous activities like skiing and parachute-jumping. "If you ask accident-prone skiers if they are scared when they are on a high-risk slope, they'll say they wouldn't bother to ski the slope if they weren't scared," said Seymour Epstein, a psychologist at the University of Massachusetts. "They want a slope that terrifies them. Parachuters say the same thing. After you take the plunge there's an immense relief and sense of well-being in facing a fear that doesn't materialize." We look for an out-of-body experience, to disconnect body, self and mind. We expect all to reunite afterward.

I am not one of those people who willingly seek to be unsettled. To me, life itself provides enough freefall. I am cautious. When I ski, I zig zag methodically and slowly. I avoid horror films. I'm done with roller coasters. And yet, I will admit to admiring thrill-seekers. A few summers ago, at Funland in Rehoboth Beach, Delaware, my kids and their younger cousin had just begun their ride on the Freefall, had strapped in and risen to the ride's zenith, when all power went out on the boardwalk, and they were caught at the top, stuck. They sat for a while, then the ride operator lowered them manually, slowly, and we walked away, grounded. I shared their disappointment, missed watching fear electrify them.

On the last day of 2012—New Year's Eve—while other children walked around town banging the resolution gong, writing down bad habits and regrets on popsicle sticks then burning them in a bonfire, eating kettle corn, and whizzing down the Russian ice slide, our friends were taking their eight-year-old son to the emergency room. Earlier in the day, he had seemed mildly sick, had just begun to complain of a sore throat, but then his fever spiked and he became suddenly worse. The doctors did not know what was going on—meningitis?—but they did not like what they saw and put him on a helicopter to Hershey Medical Center. The parents drove several tense hours to meet up with him there, and when they arrived, the doctors told them, "We're sorry. He didn't make the flight."

In the end, it turned out that Mack died of a rare blood infection. A fluke. No one could have done anything. Even if we could all travel back in time, we could not affect the outcome. And yet I still wanted to shriek: Please! Rewind!

The next week when our church youth group talked about the sudden loss of this boy, one of our own, one girl described what she felt when she heard the news: "you know that feeling you get in your stomach when you're on the amusement park ride, the Freefall?" I nodded: fear, adrenaline, and the flood of well-being when everything returns to normal.In this case, though, the freefall would not bottom out, would remain a sickening, endless feeling of howling emptiness and loss. There would be no reunion of body and spirit. No recovery from a fear that didn't materialize. Another girl talked about how Mack was not gone but transformed, like a caterpillar's transformation to butterfly, from earthbound to winged. Mack's older sister said he went to heaven on a helicopter.

In the year following their son's death, Mack's parents used words like parachutes against their freefall, weaving together their own words and those of others, like American writer and theologian Frederick Beuchner, who wrote: "Here is the world. Beautiful and terrible things will happen. Don't be afraid."

What is life at its essence, I wonder, but a rushing of wind and time against our skin, with clouds and birds and leaves and people spinning past? Even when we are sitting very still, trying not to take up more than our share of space and air, trying to avoid risk, breathing shallowly and willing everything to stay the same, we are in freefall. Best then to "turn our fall into a voluntary act," fully extend ourselves to catch the wind and to slow the disorienting spiral, calming our need to know how and where we will land.

Alison Condie Jaenicke teaches writing and literature at Penn State University, where she also serves as Assistant Director of the Creative Writing Program. Alison has earned prizes for her poems, essays, and stories, which have appeared in such publications as *Superstition Review*, *Gargoyle Magazine*, *Brain, Child*, *Literary Lunch*, and *Literary Mama*. Alison earned her BA and MA in English from the University of Virginia and currently lives in State College, PA, with her husband and two children

Annie Crow Knoll: Sunset
Gail Priest

A few days later, June heard the familiar voice in her head as she sat alone in No Name Cottage. *Fall asleep and never feel the pain again. Slide into the subterranean, seductive waters of painlessness. Nothingness. Take the step, make the decision. Let go, let go.*

The water rose up like a lover, beckoning for her to come into his arms. *I'll take it all away.* The voice was sexy, soothing.

I mustn't listen, June told herself. *I'm sitting in the living room. I'm not in the water.*

Then the lover became disturbed. The waters began to swirl. She felt the strong sucking at her feet. A vortex of energy pulled at her body. Angry now, the voice raged at her. *Come in now.* Its roar vibrated in her head and in her chest. She grabbed hold of the chair arms, her fingers white and her knuckles red with pressure.

A sudden knock at the screen door made the water recede behind the old plaster walls. The room became quiet. The knock again.

Then June heard her own voice. "Yes?"

"Hello, I'm looking for June."

Letting go of her grip on the chair arms, June forced herself to focus.

"Just a minute." She spoke barely above a whisper and stood slowly, walking onto the porch where the heat hit her.

A bald-headed woman was outside her porch door. "Hi, I hope I'm not disturbing you."

"No." June took a few steps toward the door.

"Did I wake you from a nap?"

"No. Yes."

"I'm sorry. I can come over another time." But the woman didn't move.

June waded through the thick air and pushed the screen door open. "Please come in."

"I'm Beth Ann Jakimowitz. My mom and I just got in late last night. We're from Cockatiel Cottage."

She shook June's hand. June felt energy and heat in the woman's grip.

"Mom and your mother-in-law are old friends," she continued. "I played with Nate when we were kids. Well, I followed Nate around really. He was a couple years older."

"He's not here right now." June realized that the woman was her own age. She looked at her bald head again.

"Kind of shocking, isn't it?" Beth Ann said.

"I'm sorry. I didn't mean to stare."

"It's okay. I'm used to it."

"Nate won't be back for a while."

"Good. I came to meet you. Aunt Annie told me that Nate and his wife were in No Name. I wanted to see who had landed him."

"Like a fish?"

"I thought that he was quite a catch. Just about every girl on the Knoll had a crush on him, especially Chatty Cathy from Tockwogh Cottage. You'd better keep an eye on her even now." Beth Ann winked.

"You call her Chatty Cathy, too?"

"Well, she's been talking since she was born and rarely comes up for air."

June suddenly came to and smiled. She felt an instant connection with this woman. "Sit down, won't you? Can I get you some iced tea?"

"That'd be great." Beth Ann followed her into the kitchen.

June noticed how messy everything must look to this stranger and wished Beth Ann had stayed out on the porch. None of the glasses were clean so June started washing two from the pile in the sink.

"I'm sorry this place is such a mess."

"Are you kidding? This is nothing compared to the damage I can do." Beth Ann laughed, an easy, open laugh. "And I never make my bed because I like to keep all my options open."

June smiled again. It felt strange and familiar at the same time. She poured tea over ice in the two clean glasses.

Beth Ann sat at the kitchen table by the window overlooking the east side of the Knoll toward Cattail. The tide was coming in, and her eyes followed the flow up river.

"Nate was amazing." Beth Ann spoke as if watching him out on the beach.

"What do you mean?" June set the glasses down and joined her neighbor at the table.

"He was strong and smart and cute."

"Cute?"

"Yeah, you know what I mean. He never went through an awkward stage."

June didn't interrupt. She liked hearing about her husband as a youngster.

"He had a sense of himself and what he wanted at an early age. A lot like his mom, I guess."

"You mean opinionated." June took a sip of her tea.

"Exactly."

"I'm sorry. That sounded rude." June added some sugar to her glass.

"Not at all. Just truthful. Both Nate and Aunt Annie have strong personalities." Beth Ann noticed the jars of sea glass lining the kitchen windowsills. "You've got quite a glass collection going here."

"Some of it was left behind by the former tenants, but I've found a lot, too. I want to do something with it," June admitted.

"Really? I have jars and jars of the stuff sitting over in Cockatiel Cottage from when I was a kid. What are you going to do with yours?"

"I'm not sure. A mural, I think."

"Aunt Annie said you studied art in college."

"Design. I was an interior designer." June felt good describing herself as something.

"Where?"

"What?'

"Where will you do the mural?"

"I'm not really sure that I'm doing it yet."

"Of course you are," Beth Ann said without a doubt. "So where?"

June noticed that Beth Ann didn't look at her as though she were broken or needed to be fixed. "I've been checking out the walls in the cement landing with the fireplace."

"You mean 'the pit?'"

"I guess so."

"That would be perfect."

"I don't know if Nate's mother will approve."

"Of course she will. Let's go ask her." Beth Ann stood.

"I don't have enough glass yet." June was desperate to stop the strong current Beth Ann was creating.

"Sure you do. Between what you've managed to collect so far and years and years of what my mom and brother and I have collected, you're all set."

"Yours?"

"If you want it. Plus, more washes up every day." Beth Ann walked toward the door.

She was going too quickly for June to keep up.

"There's an amazing mosaic mural with all kinds of stuff in cement on one whole side of a building in San Diego," Beth Ann said. "Would you want some old pottery and pieces of dishes and stuff?"

"You have all that in Cockatiel Cottage, too?"

"No, but I know where we can get it. There's an old dump out in the woods behind Cattail. Nate may have to cut a path for us with a machete but there's tons of broken china plates and cups and old bottles out there."

"This may sound like a stupid question, but how do you know about it?"

"Some of the old-timers used to hunt out there. I guess people still do in the fall and winter. When we were kids, we used to hike back there to dig around for treasures."

"How do you know it hasn't been picked clean?"

"Nobody goes back there."

"The hunters?"

"They're looking for deer, not broken Fiesta plates. Come on, let's go talk to Aunt Annie." Beth Ann was out the door now.

June sat frozen. Nate had told her that Aunt Grace and her ill daughter were coming to the Knoll. Beth Ann seemed anything but sick. She appeared to have more energy than a kid. June was quickly regretting having shared her idea with this pushy woman. It hadn't been anything more than a whim. She hadn't even mentioned it to Nate. Now Beth Ann wanted to get Annie's permission, and if she approved, June would actually be expected to do it. She'd have to finish it, too. That meant staying alive at least as long as it took to complete and that could be all summer.

"Let's go, June Bug." Beth Ann poked her head back in the doorway. "This is the best idea I've heard in ages. I want to help you. I won't interfere with your vision. I'll assist. I can mix mortar or whatever you use, and I can clean the glass and china."

June had trouble remembering a time when anyone took her so seriously. Beth Ann wasn't questioning her idea. She wasn't warning her to be careful or doubting her ability. So when Beth Ann started across the lawn toward Sunrise Cottage, June followed.

* * * * *

Over in Sunrise Cottage, Annie held Grace's hand as they sat together in the living room.

"I hoped Beth Ann would agree to see a doctor in Baltimore once we got here," Grace said with pain in her voice. "I have three excellent referrals, but when I brought it up this morning, she was adamant. No more treatments. Nothing except for pain management. Just the bay, the breeze, the sun and Cockatiel Cottage."

"Give her a few days to enjoy herself here. You two just arrived last night." Annie tried to sound reassuring.

"It won't make a difference. She's so sick and tired of the cures being worse than the cancer that she's just giving up." Grace slipped her hand free from Annie's hand to dab at her swollen eyes with a tissue.

Annie patted Grace's knee. There was nothing she could say.

"Thank you," Grace whispered.

"For what?" Annie gently asked.

"For not telling me I shouldn't cry. I've had to be so strong in front of Pete and Beth Ann and her brother. It feels good to just let loose."

Annie put her arms around Grace and let her cry.

Suddenly Beth Ann burst in the front door and immediately saw that her mother's eyes were red.

"Oh, Mom."

Grace averted her attention to the tissue box, took another one and blew her nose.

Beth Ann joked, "You crying over some romance novel again, Mom?"

Grace let out a laugh of relief. Once she wiped her eyes, she noticed a pale blonde standing just inside the door and recognized her as Nate's timid wife. "June, it's nice to see you again."

"I'm sorry. Have we met before?" June tried to recall this woman's face.

"I was at your wedding."

"Forgive me for not remembering."

"That's all right. I don't remember half the people at my wedding either," Grace said.

Beth Ann interrupted. "June's got a great idea."

"What's that?" Annie turned to her daughter-in-law.

June knew that she must have looked like a kindergarten child who'd forgotten the lines to her part in the class play.

Beth Ann chimed in. "She wants to do a mosaic mural on the walls of the fireplace pit."

June held her breath, anticipating the questions, the disapproval, and the doubts.

However, Annie's face lit up. "That's a wonderful idea."

"Isn't it?" Beth Ann stood next to June. "I'm going to take her back to the old dump in the woods to find china and bottles."

"It's pretty overgrown this time of year," Annie remarked.

"Nate will cut us a path." Beth Ann seemed sure he would, even though she hadn't actually seen him yet.

"Well, you'd better cover up and check every inch of your body for ticks. We don't want you getting Lyme disease." Grace gave her daughter a worried look.

"Who, me?" Beth Ann said wryly. "I defy any tick to survive the chemicals in my body, and if they don't kill the ticks, the cancer will."

"Beth Ann." Her mother didn't appreciate that kind of talk.

June laughed. She liked Beth Ann's dark sense of humor.

"But we'll make sure our June Bug here is well protected." Beth Ann threw her arm around June's shoulders.

No one but June's beloved grandfather had ever called her June Bug. He had been the one family member who pampered yet hadn't spoiled her. He'd given June her first set of paints on her ninth birthday right before he died.

"You're welcome to all our sea glass." Grace looked relieved that her daughter was excited about the project.

"Mine, too, and you might be able to get some out of Packard. But most of his are antique. I'm not sure he'll part with any." Annie smiled.

Everyone's enthusiasm made June nervous. She couldn't fathom why they were so sure she should do this.

"You give Nate a list of any supplies you need," Annie told June as she and Beth Ann were about to head down to take measurements of the walls surrounding the cement landing and stone fireplace. "You know, whatever you use to glue the stuff onto the wall, or do you set it right in mortar?"

June didn't know. "I've never done this before." She hoped that finally everyone would come to their senses, as people usually did with her, and tell her, "Oh, you'd better not try that."

But Annie didn't question anything.

"I've read about mosaic murals and saved the articles and bought two books, but they're all in storage," June explained.

Her mother-in-law didn't seem to care that June had no clue what she was doing. There wasn't even a "Before you do an entire set of walls, why not try something smaller like a glass votive."

Instead Annie seemed to accept this plan to transform the pit. "Go over to Packard's studio. He has art books on everything imaginable over there. I'm sure he'll be happy to loan you whatever you need."

"Let's get the measurements done, first." Beth Ann put on a baseball cap to protect her hairless scalp from the sun.

When they reached the landing located halfway down the cement steps to the beach, Beth Ann held one end of the tape measure while June, in her usual wide brim hat, walked to the edge of the six-foot high wall next to the fireplace. "It's seven feet and two inches long."

"Do you need me to write it down?" Beth Ann hadn't thought to bring a pencil and paper.

"No, I'll remember it."

June had always had a gift for recalling measurements. Since her depression, she had difficulty with her memory, but she felt an old confidence returning.

"What ya doing?" a little voice asked.

It was Chatty Cathy's daughter coming up from the beach. Soon her mother and two brothers followed her.

"Miss June is going to cover these walls with sea glass and shells and all kinds of pretty things." Beth Ann knelt next to Molly.

"What's that?" The little girl pointed to the tape measure.

"We're trying to see how big the walls are to know how much stuff it will take to cover them."

"You can have this." The child opened her sandy palm to reveal five pieces of smooth glass.

June walked over. "Oh, honey, you don't have to give up your treasures."

"You can have all the boxes of it we have up in Tockwogh Cottage," Cathy said. "There's glass up there from when I was her age. It'd be nice to see it become something else, especially art."

June felt a newfound respect for Cathy that left her stunned.

"Thanks, Cathy," Beth Ann replied.

"Come on, kids, time to get cleaned up." Cathy moved her small army of sandy feet, beach pails and wet towels up the steps.

As June and Beth Ann began the next measurement, Maizie appeared at the top of the stairs. "Heard you were doing a mural down there."

"News travels fast on the Knoll." Beth Ann grinned at June.

"I've got an old set of china dishes that's just collecting dust in Sunset Cottage. I'd like to see it used if you want to break it up."

Beth Ann turned to June who shook her head and took the tape to measure the height of the wall across from the fireplace.

"Thanks, Dr. Maizie. We'll take it," Beth Ann told her.

"Why did you say we'd take it? I hate to break up her good dishes." June handed Beth Ann the tape and began pulling the line to get the height of this shorter wall.

"People will want their memories immortalized in your creation. You're going to get all kinds of donations." Beth Ann's eyes sparkled with excitement.

"But I just don't want them to be disappointed after sacrificing their possessions."

"How could they be disappointed?" Beth Ann looked up at the top of the hill and saw Nate standing there watching them. He immediately smiled at her, and she felt a warmth filling her chest. He looked wonderful in his jeans and T-shirt. *Why did clothes have to fit this man so well?* The wind blew his sun-streaked hair. She knew he'd smell like the water when he got close.

"Hey, you two. What are you up to?" Nate walked down the stairs to the pit.

"Haven't you heard? Your wife's brilliant idea is the talk of the Knoll."

"Actually, I did hear." He seemed pleased to see June and his old friend working together.

Beth Ann felt her heart beating as he moved toward her.

"Good to see you, Beth Ann." Nate hugged her tight, and his embrace felt reassuring.

"You, too, Nate."

Nate turned to give June a kiss on the cheek. She avoided him.

"Where have you been all day?" she questioned in a tone that Beth Ann couldn't help but notice.

Used to June's sometimes-paranoid behavior, Nate kept his voice soft. "The toilet is cracked in Sun-swept. I had to go buy a new one. Have to get it in now so Birdie's grandkids aren't trooping into Maizie's all night to use her bathroom."

"It's after three o'clock," June noted.

"I ran into an old friend. My boss from my first restaurant job, actually."

Beth Ann remembered that Nate had had a relationship with that woman.

June busied herself measuring the wall along the steps going on down to the beach.

Beth Ann shifted the topic. "We require your services tomorrow."

"Oh, yeah?"

"We need you to get us over to the old dump to look for broken china and stuff."

"When tomorrow?" he asked.

"Late morning is best for me. I need time to get going when I first get up, and then by afternoon, I'm usually crashing. In fact, this is the longest I've been up in forever."

"I'm sorry you're sick, Beth Ann." Nate looked into her eyes.

"Yeah, it sucks. But I'm still here."

"I'm glad you're here—on the Knoll."

"Me, too. Feels right.

Nate hugged her again. "I'm sorry I lost touch with you."

"Time is funny. In some ways, it seems like only yesterday." Beth laughed. "But I've got to go lie down for a little while. June, you'll have to go over to Mr. Packard's without me."

"That's fine."

"You want me to walk you up?" Nate offered.

"No, I'll make it." Beth Ann disappeared up the stairs.

June suddenly sat on the cement step where she'd been measuring the wall.

"Are you all right?" Nate moved toward her.

June nodded.

"Do you want me to go with you to Packard's?"

June shook her head.

"Okay then, I'll get to work on that toilet."

"Nate?" June said quickly.

"Yes?"

"Nothing."

* * * * *

June had wanted to see Packard's Schoolhouse Studio ever since she'd arrived on the Knoll several weeks ago. Now she had an excuse to go. As she walked across the field, she was glad in the end that the gregarious Beth Ann wasn't with her. Although she had taken an instant liking to her, June wanted the opportunity to raise the kinds of questions she longed to ask about Packard's work without interruption.

She greatly admired the paintings Nate had taken her to see in both Philadelphia and New York City galleries. Nate had even purchased one of Packard's abstracts for a prominent wall in the bistro. June hoped he hadn't sold that to Charlie along with his half of the business.

After making her way up the Schoolhouse Studio steps, which were edged with pots of yellow, orange and red nasturtiums, June found the large double wooden doors were open. Since the outer screens were closed, she didn't want to walk right in, so she knocked lightly on the wooden frame of one of the doors.

* * * * *

Packard had a vague awareness of a woodpecker thumping away on a tree outside his studio. When he painted, not much of the outside world penetrated his concentration. The thumping sound started up again, and it wasn't the right rhythm for a Northern Flicker or Red-bellied Woodpecker. The noise alerted Packard to the environment around him and outside his painting.

"Yes?" he called out, realizing a person was knocking at the door. He rubbed his hands and then his brush on a rag and set it in the mason jar of linseed oil.

"Hello?" June   glanced down as she stood at the door.

"Hi, June, I've been expecting you." He pushed open one of the screen doors.

"Did you hear about the mosaic mural I'm doing?" she asked as he ushered her through the door.

"No."

June made eye contact. "You said that you were expecting me?"

"I have been for some time. Welcome to the Schoolhouse Studio."

"Thank you."

The studio was a dream to June: the smell of paints and linseed oil; brushes lined up in jars on various makeshift tables; blank canvases stretched and stacked in racks against the walls; shelves filled with art books; an old utility sink lined with stains from every painting ever created in this room. But it was much more than that. It was a sanctuary. The rising afternoon heat moved the two large mobiles of crows and planets hanging in the rafters. June didn't know where to turn first.

"Am I disturbing you?" she asked.

"Not at all. I wanted you to see these." Packard gestured to two recently completed paintings of bay scenes. "Since you arrived, I've been painting water scenes. I've spent my entire life fishing. Aside from your mother-in-law's family, I knew mostly watermen. And yet, I hadn't painted them. It astounds me when I ponder it. Living and working on the bay, but I hadn't focused solely on it until now."

June looked carefully at the first completed piece. The view was over the shoulders of two men pulling crab traps onto the deck of their workboat. The water surrounding the boat was just as June saw it with layers of white, gray, and various shades of blue. Somehow Packard made the light refract right off the canvas. It was the water that called to her in her darkest moments.

As if reading her mind, Packard spoke again. "When I noticed the way you look at the bay, I was obligated to see it again, new."

"I've never seen water like this in a painting. It's more real than artists can capture. Aiken's water isn't this wet."

"Thanks."

"I want to slip right into it and float away."

"But you're creating a mosaic mural instead." There was no question in Packard's voice.

"Apparently, unless you can convince me otherwise."

"Why would I want to do that?"

"Someone should, and you seem to be the one with the most sense around here."

Packard laughed. June had a sense of humor. He was quickly noticing the things that must have drawn Nate to her in the first place. There had to be attributes beyond the initial chemistry between young people. June was lovely in a pale, vulnerable way, and she was bright, too.

"Nate's mom mentioned that you might have some books on mosaics?"

"I'm sure there's something here." He motioned to a case of books and walked toward them. "Let's have a look."

"Thanks." Hanging on the wall next to the bookcase was another of Packard's paintings, a winter landscape. June stopped to examine it. Standing in the snow-filled woods, a white buck stared out at her with his pink eyes.

"Is it an albino deer?" she asked.

Packard nodded. "They're rare."

June chuckled and then noticed the surprise in Packard's eyes. "'Albino' was a nickname some of the kids gave me when I was little. They thought it was funny. I was so pale and with this practically white hair." She pulled at one of her platinum blonde strands.

"In my grandmother's day, women carried parasols to block the sun. Pale was preferable."

"Maybe I was born in the wrong decade."

As Packard removed several dusty books from the shelves, June carried them to a nearby table.

"I'm interrupting your painting."

"It'll keep."

"No, I can look through these. Please paint, if you want."

"Okay."

June liked sitting on a stool at the large wooden table thumbing through the half dozen books on the history and application of mosaics. There were three books on contemporary murals, and two had information specifically on outdoor preparation.

"Have you done any mosaic murals?" June asked.

"Not yet." Pack applied fresh paint to a second pallet. "It's on the list of things to do."

"Is it a long list?"

He paused in thought. "Long enough to keep me going, but not so long to cause any regrets if I don't get to everything."

"I regret not painting," June admitted.

"That's easily remedied."

"My parents didn't approve."

"We won't tell them." He winked.

"Tell them what?"

"That you're painting."

"I am?" She stood.

He handed her the second pallet he'd just filled and a jar of brushes. He grabbed a blank canvas off a rack and placed it on the easel next to his current painting. Then he picked up his own pallet and brush and began to work.

"First water."

June began to repeat on her canvas what he was doing on his.

*   *   *   *   *

Just a few days after meeting Beth Ann, June stood alone in the pit at dawn, armed with more mosaic materials than she could use, along with glass cutters, bottle cutters, various mosaic pliers and tools, safety glasses, frost proof cement and grout guaranteed to hold well below freezing. She was reminded of the W. H. Murray quote from the Scottish Himalayan Expedition.

"That's the moment one definitely commits oneself, then Providence moves too. All sorts of things occur to help one that would never otherwise have occurred. A whole stream of events issues from the decision, raising in one's favor all manner of unforeseen incidents and meetings and material assistance which no man could have dreamed would have come his way."

People assumed that June had made the commitment, and they began to bring things she could use in the mural.

Miss Beverly, who was friendly with a potter in Chester Landing, brought rejected pieces to be used whole or broken. Also donated were pottery cones, used to gauge the temperature of the kiln, frozen in various stages of melt-down. *Perfect to surround a circle of mirror,* June thought.

When Knollers found out June was planning to use pieces of mirror so folks would see themselves in the mural, Nancy Abrams donated two large mirrors that she found at local yard sales, and Packard dug up three more from his attic. Two boxes of household china and glass arrived from Connie Renker and the Reynolds sisters. Bob and Jean Reynolds contributed forty old bottles their sons had dug up in the woods behind Cattail and along the riverbanks when they were boys.

Once Nate cleared a path to the old dump, the teenagers on the Knoll hiked out there to explore and always returned with treasures of broken pottery and china for June. Anyone willing to donate their day's scavenging from the beach or the dump could deposit their treasures in buckets Beth Ann had positioned and labeled by category and color in the pit.

Despite everyone's assumption that June was going to do this, when she mixed the cement this morning and stood with the first piece of broken chi-na, she hesitated. Holding onto that first piece of mosaic, June felt as if she were exposing her very core to the world. The minute she started, she would feel everyone's eyes on her. The criticism would begin.

To reassure herself, June had shown Packard several pages of graph paper covered with design ideas for these walls. He wasn't discouraging at all, but he hadn't been encouraging either. Neutral was what he'd been. The one thing he'd said to June was to consider working from her heart and not solely her head. That had always worked best for him.

"Hold the pieces in your hands. Let them tell you where they belong on the wall," he'd told her.

As the sun moved higher in the sky, June still stood fingering the first piece in her hand. It was a choice; hers to make. But once she began, there was no turning back because June Bidwell finished things that she started. It bothered her that she hadn't finished what she had begun in the bathroom of their Manhattan apartment. Instead, she and Nate were left with a mess to work though. She had longed for an end to the pain and confusion, only to wake up in the hospital with more chaos. What a bitter disappointment that had been.

June turned the china shard in her hand again and suddenly felt the sharp edge of it slice into her finger. A tiny drop of blood oozed out, and she felt a surge of excitement.

This was a new choice, she realized. She sucked at her cut finger, and then applied a trowel of cement to the wall and set the first piece.

Gail Priest is the author of the *Annie Crow Knoll* series. *Annie Crow Knoll: Sunrise* debuted in 2013. *Annie Crow Knoll: Sunset* was released in 2014. *Annie Crow Knoll: Moonrise* came out later in 2015. Gail's career in performing arts and education has allowed her to play various roles: teacher, adjunct college professor, guidance counselor, actor, director, and writer. Her play *Eva's Piano* was produced at the Dayton Playhouse in their 2000 New Play Festival. The Church Hill Theatre in Church Hill, Maryland staged a reading of her play *A Thing with Feathers*. Gail lives in New Jersey. She and her husband rent a cottage on the Chesapeake Bay in a cottage community that is the inspiration for the *Annie Crow Knoll* series.

Last Walk with My Sister

Susan Weaver

For Barbara

I pick up a feather, brush away the sand
as a pelican plummets into the sea.
Alone, I recall a different beach
she and I walked a year ago.
Her son, tall at sixteen, searched in seaweed

at water's edge. Again and again, he
took aim, hurled live crabs back into the surf
as our footsteps traced the breakers' white lace.
Did she hint at turmoil? I ache

to remember. Surf's roar muffled
the ebb and flow of sisters' talk.
She must have touched on work and home,
her two sons growing into manhood,
nearly strangers to me, too many states

between us. We scooped up sea snails,
spirals radiating sunset colors,
eyes at the centers of their coils
seeing perhaps more than I--

I, who thought my sister, like the tides,
would always be there. Now I scan the line
of red umbrellas leaned into the wind.
Beyond, only sea. In my hands, a feather
and sand that clings like gritty sorrow.

Susan Weaver is a poet who also answered hotline calls and assisted shelter residents for twelve years on staff at an agency for victims of domestic abuse. Twelve years ago, her family suffered its own domestic violence. Weaver's poems about those experiences have appeared in literary journals (*Juxtaposition, Main Street Rag, qaartsiluni, red lights, Schuylkill Valley Journal, Survivor*, and *Women's Way*), and the sociological journal *Violence Against Women*. Her haiku have been anthologized in *Common Wealth: Contemporary Poets on Pennsylvania* and *Unexpected Harvest: A Gathering of Blessings*. Weaver is also a travel writer, cycling journalist, and author of *A Woman's Guide to Cycling* (Ten Speed Press, rev. ed., 1998). She lives in Allentown, Pa., with her husband Joseph C. Skrapits, a painter and writer.

Animator
Elizabeth Mosier

I'll sleep after the deadline. Around me, inkers and painters sit at every drafting desk: old hands and new hires, their heads bent over celluloid sheets. Mr. Disney's movie must be ready before Christmas, our momentary masterpieces stacked and filmed and finished at the Technicolor plant.

For weeks now, I've risen every day at 5:00 o'clock, dressed for the heat in a white cotton shift, gulped a cup of Gram's strong tea, and walked a half-mile through the lemon grove to board a streetcar to Burbank. I ride with other women, domestics in aprons and slippers, and men in work boots and dungarees grasping tin lunch pails in their fat fists. The air is still and cool as we pull out of Pasadena, leaving behind the cramped bungalow, the patch of crab grass in front, the soiled rag rug in the kitchen, the sugar bowl crawling with ants my poor old Gram can't see. At that new hour, the dark palms cut across the lightening sky like ravens flying in formation. I imagine painting this backdrop on glass in rose and violet shades, as we speed forward into the day, to Hyperion Avenue and the animation studio where life begins.

In the Ink and Paint department, we don't talk. Quiet helps us concentrate, so we won't slop ink or slip up and paint the wrong side of a cel. The little we know of each other, we've learned in quick flashes during ten-minute breaks. Still, we work as one body, like a giant squid dipping its tentacles in jars of Cartoon Colour, filling in the pictures Mr. Disney dreams up and the artists draw.

Today it's POISON APPLE/Scene 12A/1 – 249. I flip over each cel and brush-stroke its backside: red for the apple, black and white and gray for the hag with her all-seeing eyes. I know how the story ends, though Gram banned fairy tales when I was small, and read to me only from the Bible. ("God loves you," she whispers to me every morning as I set off in the dark, but it's her love that binds. She banished my mother and held onto me.) Brush in hand, I think how little it would take to change the story—blot the hag's eyes shut or push the apple's outline imperceptibly to the right until it floats off the screen—but I don't. I keep my head down, working neatly and quickly as I've been trained, so the paint won't streak. Brush to jar to cel to jar, over and over and over.

I'm not beautiful, but once I was asked to pose for Snow White, to teach the young artists how real girls move. Those boys only know their own mamas, and they're so blind and boastful they can't even draw the Prince believably. They studied me with such longing, which I was too old, even then, to read as love. I see it for what it was: a wish to capture me with ink strokes on paper. As my mother was captured, but with words. *Ruined*, Gram says, by a con artist.

Brush to jar to cel to jar. This work needs a steady hand, so there's no late-night boozing with the boys for us, no jolt of coffee or full-belly breakfast for me. Hunger sharpens my focus on each frame of the story, thousands of drawings for minutes of film. Put a brush in my hand and I enter a dream; I'm both in the picture and painting it, sitting at my desk and hovering above it thinking *here I am, an animator*. I've been at it for hours when Annie, whose desk touches mine, suddenly begins to sob into her white-gloved hands. For a moment, I'm sure I've imagined it.

Carol, the bossy girl from Chicago, rushes over to help her or silence her, I can't tell which. She stands over Annie with her hands on her hips, stinking as always of cigarettes. I unwrap the buttermilk biscuits Gram packed for me, and offer Annie my handkerchief.

"He's coming back," Annie says, pulling a letter from her pocket and fanning the hellish air with it.

"Some nerve that man has," Carol says. We all know about Annie's husband, a doctor in Nogales who steals opiates from the sick and the dying. She confessed this only once, in the courtyard at noon break, but that quick glimpse was enough to set the shameful scene playing on and on in our heads. "Tell me you're not going to take him back."

"His brother's talked some sense into him," Annie says. She unfolds the letter and scans it for proof.

"For now," Carol says. "What happens when he starts up again?"

"I'm going to have a baby," Annie says and no one, not even Carol, has an answer for that.

Every girl has her deadline. She might arrive at the studio in a pressed dress and heels, but she will leave wrinkled and limping, her waistband either shrunken from stress or straining with scandal. Annie's seat will soon be empty, and the rest of us will cover for her. Brush to jar to cel to jar, Snow White reaching for the poison apple, frame by frame by frame. *God loves you*, Gram keeps calling to me through the dark.

When I interviewed for my job at the studio, my hands shook as I showed Mr. Disney my sketches of lizards and jackrabbits, watercolors of oleander bushes and lemon trees. Fatherless and penniless, I'd pinned my hope to my talent. "I have no formal training," I told him meekly, but he stopped me with a laugh.

"You're perfect," he said. "I want untrained girls. Young artists who aren't set in their ways." When he called me "artist," it was my first time. He offered me a cigarette—of course I refused, sensing a test—and slid open a heavy oak drawer containing the contracts. That moment lasted forever, like a tower of painted cels rising to the sky. On the desk between us lay my drawings, naïve and unschooled, revealing nothing so much as my willingness. Then Mr. Disney smiled and signed the contract with a flourish. When he passed it to me, I drew my name with an unbroken line: *Marjorie Green*.

Here it is then, finished, the picture of my youth: a studio girl in a clean smock and spotless gloves, sitting at a drafting desk grasping a drying brush. When I look down again at my life's work, I see that the gray paint has streaked. This is an amateur's mistake, which ruins the screen's illusion by revealing the maker's hand.

"God," I say.

"Hold on, Grandma," says the girl with pink hair, folding and tucking the white sheet around my waist. "The nurse is coming with something for the pain." Her hands smell of smoke, and her pale, plump arms are branded with Chinese dragons and Celtic scrolls. My own arms are tattooed, too—bruised where my blood has pooled in intricate patterns of branches and roots. All those years, all that ink, an enchanted forest spreading under my skin. Where are my gloves, I wonder, to keep the artwork clean?

Elizabeth Mosier is the author of *The Playgroup* (part of GemmaMedia's "Open Door" series of novellas to promote adult literacy), a novel, *My Life as a Girl* (Random House), and numerous short stories, articles, essays, and reviews. Her work has appeared most recently and is forthcoming in *The Journal of Compressed Creative Arts*, *The Dock: Hayden's Ferry Review Online*, *Cleaver*, and *Creative Nonfiction*. A graduate of Bryn Mawr College and the MFA Program for Writers at Warren Wilson College, Moiser has twice been named a Discipline Winner by the Pew Fellowships in the Arts and has received a fiction grant from the Pennsylvania Council on the Arts.

Life Cycles
J.D. Munro

1969 Honda CL 125 Scrambler, maroon and chrome, an on-off road bike with a high exhaust and skid plates: my dad's last motorcycle and my earliest memory. He took the helmetless kids on the block for rides one day. We lined up for our turn, like for a carnival ride, and we each got one lap around the long, steep block. Although I waited with impatience for my turn, I wanted the ride to end as soon as it started. My perch felt precarious. I wasn't big enough to straddle the seat, and my kindergartener's legs stuck straight out from under my mini, flower-child dress. I grabbed Dad's waist to keep me aboard, and I cherished a brief moment of physical closeness with my aloof father. This was the first and last time that I would feel small on a motorcycle's passenger seat, which tend to be the size and consistency of a toaster. We were not to mention the ride to Mom, who never went out on any of Dad's motorbikes.

Every morning, Dad took a clover-leaf freeway off-ramp on his way to work. He rode flat out in third gear, the Honda leaning sideways as he accelerated into the tight turn, popping into fourth as he exited the curve. He couldn't make himself slow down or wear a helmet. He never went down on a bike, but he felt that motorcycling was too risky once he had a family. Dad sold the bike and never bought another, although he kept his helmet for forty years. I never got another ride from him.

Two months before I met him, my husband crashed into a chain-link fence on his six-year-old motorcycle: a 1981 Suzuki Twin Turbo GS-1100, black with orange stripes and a square headlight. Among the first of the high performance bikes that gave birth to the term "crotch rocket," the bike could hit 120 mph in a ten-second quarter-mile, which is about how far Richard traveled a few hours after his submarine docked. After fifty-six days underwater, Richard had no land legs, much less the ability to steer a bike marketed as "The Speed King" through a network of cul-de-sacs. Itching for freedom and movement, he took the bike out for a quick test spin. He wore flip flops, swim trunks, a tank top, and sunglasses. No helmet. The bike left the road in a curve and hit a fence's center post head-on. The impact cracked the bike's engine casing. Richard flew up onto the top of the fence, which carved twin tracks down his scalp. The fence boomeranged him back into the center of the street, fifty feet away. I think of the cracked engine and Richard's head as the same entity, but at the time no one knew how badly his brain had been damaged. The military hospital only fixed his broken arm. He hid an abundant amount of non-regulation hair under his sailor's cap, so I guess they figured there was enough cushioning to dispense with X-rays or brain scans.

Two months after the collision, arm cast removed that day, Richard crossed on a Don't Walk to the street corner where I was standing with a friend, waiting for the Walk. "You girls look bored," he said, which I guess I was. There was something intriguingly off-kilter about him. He tried an unusual pickup tactic. He took my fingers and ran them along the Franken-stein's monster scars on his scalp, palpable even under copious eighties hair product and a stiff matt of hair. He was definitely not run-of-the-mill; most guys who've just had their brains raked probably aren't.

I believe that Richard continued to date me over the summer because he needed my dad's pickup truck to haul his 1970 Triumph Tiger 650 to a friend's garage. We were ill-matched, this moody boy and I, but he expanded my vocabulary with terms like "project bike." I thought this meant some-day riding a restored, antique motorcycle, a gorgeous and coveted object of beauty, but later I learned the true definition: doesn't run now and never will. Two months after I met him, Richard had another head injury, owing to poor decision making that turned out to be a direct result of that fence forking his brain. Those moods of his that spiraled increasingly out of con-trol led to my decision to stop dating him; they were really the symptoms of an undiagnosed and untreated Traumatic Brain Injury. He said the wrong thing at the wrong time in the wrong place to the wrong group of people, who wiped his head against the concrete and put him into a coma. When he awoke, the doctor proclaimed him a vegetable. I don't know what happened to the Triumph, which he never got started.

My brother's low rider was the biggest Harley Davidson on the market: a 1985 FXRS 1340 Low Glide blockhead. Unfortunately, it glided too low in a too-small cloverleaf just a mile from the cloverleaf Dad used to take. My brother spent the next year in and out of the hospital, undergoing six surgeries to save his arm, which is now more metal than bone. Meanwhile, I drove Richard to the same hospital a few times a week and would visit my brother while Richard learned to walk and talk again. I never had the chance to stop dating him, and, besides, he slept most of the time now, so he wasn't much trouble. Since we were already living the life of an old married couple, we got hitched.

The Navy wisely decided that it would be best to never trust Richard with steering a nuclear submarine again, but rather than lingering like an eggplant as the doctor predicted, Richard became an egghead. He surpassed me in advanced degrees and became a college teacher so that he could have summers off for motorcycle trips. After seven years together, we threw out the birth control and bought a classic bike, a 1971 BMW R75 Slash 5. It made no sense at the time, but we hadn't done anything by the book thus far. We fell over on our first tandem ride. Not far along, no permanent damage. Rather similar to the miscarriage that followed not much later. With both, we shrugged, then got back on the horse and tried again. I hadn't ridden the motorcycle while pregnant, and I never would. Although my mother thought the bike might "vibrate that baby right out of you," the doctor rolled his eyes and waved that possibility away. But I knew my literature. Holly Golightly "lost the heir" after she galloped her horse through New York City streets. A century earlier, *Middlemarch's* equally-spirited Rosamond Vincy also miscarried after saddling up, so I wouldn't tempt fate on the back of a machine with the power of fifty horses but only two hooves.

The next spring I bought my very own first motorcycle: a 1969 Honda CL 125, now called an Enduro. A gritty little all-terrain, endurance machine with studded tires that could handle mud and rocks. I knew a lot of women who'd had one miscarriage, but I didn't know any who had two like me. I'd left the beaten path and was on the road to learning a lot about endurance, but I didn't know a damn thing about manual transmissions, and this bike had no electric start. Kick-starting a motorcycle is sexy, we all know that, but it took me a dozen tries to leverage my not-insignificant weight against a peg of iron until the engine flatulated to life. Then I'd stall out as I staccatoed instead of eased out the clutch. I never left the driveway, but I developed a killer calf muscle. Not until years later did I realize this was the same bike model on which I'd taken my virgin motorcycle ride with my father.

I rode a 1994 Honda 125, a nondescript course-issued bike, for a motor-cycle safety course. With its push start button, I could fire the bike up just fine after killing the engine dozens of times throughout the morning session in a parking lot. Kind of the same with my uterus: started up a pregnancy just fine, then came that sickening lurch and halt. The teacher yelled at me over and over, "More gas! More gas! More gas!" By midday, I still could not get the bike to move forwards more than a couple of inches, helped along by my feet more than the engine. Fed up with being at the bottom of the class for the first time in my perfect GPA life, I gave it more gas and popped a wheelie, picking up a surprising amount of speed in first gear as I headed on one tire for the chain link fence that surrounded the parking lot. I wore a helmet, so I would not sport a twin scalp to my husband's. Still, a spectacular ricochet off the fence looked imminent just as I pulled in the clutch. The motorcycle lowered itself and tapped the earth, and I stopped a few feet short of impact without cutting the engine. I completed the lap, then quit the class. I clearly had no aptitude for a sport disguised as transportation, which required as much testosterone as coordination, of which I had neither.

I learned to work a clutch on an old sports car Richard bought for me after I nearly died with an ectopic pregnancy. Teaching me to operate the car's manual transmission, Richard practiced the infinite patience he'd thought he wouldn't need until we had a teenager. Since I could now work a gear shift, and since I'd also lost some of my female organs along with the baby, perhaps I could now be ballsy enough to man-handle a bike. I signed up again for the motorcycle riding course and passed it on the course-issued 1995 Honda 125, this time with no unintentional stunts.

I earned my motorcycle license on a 1983 Yamaha Exciter 185cc, electric blue (faded). I weaved around cones that a Harley rider knocked over one after the other, like a drunk bear trampling a row of tulips. I loved this bike, but grannies with shopping carts could pass me on the road on that little machine. I sold it prematurely, wanting something bigger and more powerful, which I guess comes with the territory of boy toys.

We bought a bullet-nosed, fiberglass, detachable Harley sidecar, scuffed black, for Richard's bike. For a dog, as it turned out.

After the latest pregnancy loss, feeling antsy, Richard decided to take a motorcycle cross-country. I had no desire for more discomfort and unknowns, so I would remain home, hopefully gestating yet another attempt at parenthood. The vintage BMW was too unreliable for the journey, so Richard bought a dark green, 1994 Yamaha Virago 750cc, a barely-used bike with 498 miles on the odometer. I noticed a lot of barely-used bikes for sale. Lots of people quit early in the game. It just wasn't as easy as it looked.

I got more looks in one week on my next bike than I had in three decades on foot: a 1994 Kawasaki Eliminator 250. Sleek, black with red piping, powerful, another barely-used bike. With a low-end torque and narrow speed band, I shifted four times by the time it hit twenty. Few certainties in life compared to the feel of my boot-toe pressing down on the gear shift, the subsequent chunking of shifting gears, their popping into place that settled in my joints. I craved the visceral sense of control, the sure cause and effect, the transference of power from bone to metal back to vibrating bone. Then the bike would hit its stride and take off on its own. After another miscarriage, I decided last-minute to join Richard on his cross-country trip, but on my own bike. This bike wasn't big enough, either. After nearly hitting a tree on a practice run and killing my engine in the middle of a six-lane highway, I realized that riding my own motorcycle would handily solve our fertility problem because I would kill myself. While I loved to shift, I never found the confidence to lean into turns. In the end, I made the practical choice and rode cross-country on the back of Richard's bike. For the record, let's please call that chrome arch behind me a back rest rather than a sissy bar. If I'm riding at all, I'm no sissy.

We had nothing left to prove after twenty-six states and 10,000 miles on a bike that everyone said would be too small. Scaling down our expectations to a 1962 Sears Allstate scooter 49cc seemed like a good idea. It was a cycle originally sold out of a department store catalog. The 49cc engine must have been giving the finger to some old regulation—or else why not 50cc? Perhaps the one extra cubic centimeter of power would have promoted it from a catalog toy to an adult machine. Cubic centimeter is simply the amount of power, but in reality cc as the measuring unit of displacement is as complicated as the miraculous, tricky, and perfect timing of cell division required of an embryo.

So we already had four cycles. But how could Richard resist a beautiful bike, the man's version of retail therapy after a fifth miscarriage? He bought a 1967 Triumph Bonneville 750 from a friend. The owner, Theo, a quirky jeweler, designed a tenth-anniversary necklace that Richard surprised me with. Theo had engraved the engine casings with a Tom Pinion 1600's clock design of thistles, leaves, and vines. Hey, if you're going to tattoo yourself, you might as well tattoo your bike. Second definition of Project Bike: motorcycle that doesn't run, sold from friend to friend to friend in order to decorate a succession of garages. A bike that gives a gaggle of guys something to stare at while drinking beer rather than looking each other in the eye and having a meaningful conversation about, say, one's thwarted desire to become a father. They talk instead about strokes, pistons, and thrust.

A rider should be able to set her feet flat on the ground, which I could do with very few bikes. Our next Project Bike was meant for me: a 1965

Honda Superhawk 305, silver. The Superchicken, as we fondly dubbed it, fit me perfectly, but Richard never found the energy to get it running well. We were both tired. Sold to the same friend who bought the Bonneville. This motorcycle merry-go-round started to feel like me, passed from doctor to doctor to doctor.

By coincidence, our next bike was a 1957 Lambretta 125cc scooter, the same make my father rode home from swing shift at the Pearl Harbor machine shop when I was a baby because it was the only reliable form of transportation Dad could afford. About forty years later, ours was a rare basket case. Basket Case meant all of the parts were there but not assembled. Alternate definition for Basket Case: me after six miscarriages. Something simply wasn't firing right.

We liked to have more motorbikes than miscarriages. The Banana was a bright-yellow 1996 Honda scooter; it brought us up to seven bikes, and soon the numbers would even up again. More dangerous than the Speed King because it was too slow, this bike topped out at thirty-five downhill with a tailwind. Still, we finally paired up on separate bikes for frequent, unpretentious rides around town together on the Sears scooter and the Banana. We whined around town together most weekends one happy summer, keeping to side streets. We blew white smoke, watching for kids and cats, never getting farther than three miles from home. We no longer knew where we were going, so puttering close to home was best.

Our first and only brand new bike sat on the showroom floor for three years before Richard bought it. True to clichés about men, this bike has since become highly-coveted now that it's no longer being produced. I get that, because I know what it's like to want something you can't have. The 1999 Kawasaki Vulcan 1500 Drifter was a replica of a 1940 Indian, red and white with full, flaring fenders: our prettiest bike, our biggest bike, and what we knew would be our last bike, on which we would take our last long trip. We went slow and didn't cover much ground. The shocks were unique to this bike because of the rear suspension; the back fender floats with the rear tire. Friends tailing us told us it was remarkable to watch, but I never saw it, being on top of it. We sold all the bikes except this one, but planned to sell it soon. We were now certified for adoption and in the child-search phase. Our social worker regularly sent us write-ups and pictures of children needing homes.

Our six-year-old son arrived. Therapists and social workers later told us that with his severe behaviors, any other family would have turned him back over to the state. Eleven other families already had. Not that the thought didn't occur to us, but we hung on. We'd never sought untarnished perfection. Our marriage started with a crash and a coma, so we knew about perseverance.

Meanwhile, Richard's mother backed over the Drifter and dented the gas tank and crash bars. A windstorm knocked the bike over and cracked the headlight casing. In order to sell the bike, Richard had it towed to the shop to fix a mysterious electrical problem (which turned out to be a dead battery), but it fell off the tow truck. The spill cracked the front fender and studded leather seat and further dented the crash bars. When the Drifter returned from the shop with a new battery and an ugly crack in its once gorgeous, flaring fender, Richard bought some liquid fiberglass and patched it up. He wrapped a leather tank bag around the dented tank. He couldn't bring himself to sell it.

We bought a 1983 Honda Goldwing Aspencade with double-wide Family Touring sidecar, for dog and son.

Theo, the jeweler, lost his wife to cancer. In their years together, his wife refused to ride any of his motorcycles with him. Now he was selling everything to take an old boat around the world by himself. Richard thought Theo's 1983 BMW 650 was the perfect bike for me. I'd been dropping hints about my own wheels again. Richard took it for a test drive while I talked to Theo, and our son played with a pile of parts. Theo missed his wife. He could talk of nothing else but her, their long marriage, her death. I watched Richard ride off down the street. He never looked more content than when cradled in the saddle of a motorcycle.

Theo gave Richard the key so he could ride the BMW whenever he wanted while making up his mind. I knew this wasn't the bike for me, but I could tell Richard wanted it. I wouldn't refuse him. Everyone tells us that motorcycles are dangerous. They are. But what if I had refused them all those years ago? Pressed together in the space the size of a dresser drawer, we journeyed on as a pair.

One day when I was out for a walk a couple of miles from home, Richard unknowingly rode past me on the dented and cracked Drifter, our (helmeted) son tucked behind him, arms tight around his dad's waist, magically floating. He told me later that he felt like he was going to fall off. Then, he asked his Dad when they could go riding again.

J. D. Munro is a freelance editor whose online column, *Straight-No-Chaser Mom*, is the First Place winner in the 2015 National Society of Newspaper Columnists blog competition. She was a Top Ten Finalist in the Erma Bombeck Global Humor Competition. Her numerous publishing credits include: *Salon*; *Brainchild*; *Gulf Coast*; *North American Review*; *Best American Erotica*; and *The Bigger the Better the Tighter the Sweater: 21 Funny Women on Beauty and Body Image*. Her humorous stories about sex and the sexes are collected in *The Erotica Writer's Husband*.

Aller Simple

Tina Pisco

for Amelia

I bought a one-way ticket
for the first time in my life.
Aller Simple. No return;

and felt deep in my heart
strings snap as I knew they would

the minute they handed you
to me, I knew
someday you'd leave.

And so tried to remember,

to savour, to cherish
to relish the flavour
of each passing hour

of each passing day
of each passing year
that brought us closer to that parting.

I bought a one-way ticket
for the first time in my life.
Aller Simple. A simple go

and sent you on your way-

Ma petite fille.
Ma petite cherie,
mon Amelie.

Tina Pisco is 57 years old and has been a professional writer for over thirty years. She has written for all mediums except radio. She has published two novels, a collection of newspaper columns, and a poetry collection, as well as articles, screenplays, short stories, and flash fiction. A collection of her short stories will be published by Fish Publishing in 2016. Though born an American, Tina Pisco grew up in a multicultural, trilingual family, in a number of European countries. She has lived in rural West Cork, Ireland for the past twenty years, where she has raised four daughters, numerous pets, and lots of vegetables.

Ties That Bind

Nancy Kotkin

Sophia crawls under her bed to retrieve her other sneaker and jams it on her foot. She needs to hurry. Downstairs, her mother and father are already yelling at each other.

"Where's my grandfather's silk tie?"

"I sold some of our old junk last week."

"You bastard! That tie was an heirloom. It was the only thing I had left from Papa. He got married in that tie. You had no right to sell it."

"I don't need your stinkin' permission to do what I see fit in my own household. Do you think it's easy to pay the bills with you sitting around at home?"

Sophia tiptoes through the living room. Her mother shoves her father with both her hands against his chest.

"I'm *not* 'sitting around' at home. I'm raising your children. Do you think it's easy to do the laundry, chauffeur the kids, help with homework –"

"You don't have a god damn job. What else have you got to do while I bust my ass supporting you?"

Sophia beelines towards the back door. Best to get away before the hitting starts.

"Where are you going?" calls her mother.

"To play at Brandon's house."

"Make sure you're home in time for dinner," warns her father.

Sophia slams the back door, shutting out her parents.

She lets out her breath in the quiet play room at Brandon's. "Let's play Chutes and Ladders."

"Nah. We always play that."

"We could watch *Finding Nemo*." Sophia picks up her favorite movie and hands it to Brandon.

"We just saw that yesterday."

"So what do you want to do then?"

"I know! Let's get married like my aunt did last week."

"No, I don't want to."

"Come on, Sophia. Marry me."

Sophia shakes her head vigorously from side to side. "I'm never getting married."

Brandon crosses his arms over his chest. "If you won't marry me, I don't want to play with you anymore."

Faced with the prospect of going home, Sophia caves in. "Oh, okay."

Brandon beams and starts right in on preparations for their marriage ceremony. "Let's go outside and pick your flowers." Sophia wanders the yard aimlessly while Brandon pulls every dandelion he can find.

Then they sneak into his parents' walk-in closet. Brandon takes a black suit jacket off a hanger and selects a grey silk tie for himself. He looks over his mother's dresses until he pulls out a fancy white one. "Here, Sophia, you wear this."

Sophia wrinkles her nose at his selection.

Brandon puts a hand on his hip. "You have to wear a wedding dress to get married."

Sophia pulls the dress haphazardly over her head. "Who's going to marry us?"

"I'll ask my brother to be the minister."

Outside, Sophia wobbles up in high heels, clutching her bouquet of dandelions.

"I now pronounce you man and wife till death do you part." Brandon's brother scampers off, calling over his shoulder, "You're supposed to kiss the bride now."

Brandon looks over at the scowling Sophia. "We could skip that part. Throw your bouquet."

Sophia hurls her dandelions into the wind. As they scatter into the air, she wishes she could fly away with them. "Now can we watch *Finding Nemo*?"

Brandon shrugs. "Yeah, I guess."

They return to the play room where Brandon picks up *Tarzan*. "Let's watch this instead."

"I want to see *Finding Nemo*." Sophia shoves Brandon so hard he ricochets off the far wall. She stomps over to him and yanks him by the tie.

Rubbing his neck, Brandon asks, "Hey, what'd you do that for?"

"We're married now. I'm being your wife."

Nancy Kotkin is the owner, instructor, and editor of *Brave New Words*. She writes fiction and screenplays, primarily for children and young adults. She has won first place at the 2010 & 2014 Philadelphia Writers' Conferences for excerpts from different novels. She is fervently pursuing her MFA in Creative Writing and MA in Publishing, both from Rosemont College.

Nancy has previously taught at Temple University, Rosemont College, and various community colleges. In addition, she has spoken at numerous regional and national conferences on topics related to e-learning and instructional design. Nancy is the former president of the Philadelphia Metro Chapter of the Society for Technical Communication (STC) and was a founding board member of the PA/NJ/DE chapter of the United States Distance Learning Association (USDLA).

Bone House

Anne Kaier

Saint Jerome often ponders near an ancient skull, polished
like a vase. Something to symbolize mortality.
But after many years, doesn't the skull become
familiar? An artifact lying around, keeping him company?
Does he ever scrub his thumb across the jagged edges of the nose
or does he just pat the thing, admire the way its curves
complement a water jug?
If death is your familiar, doesn't it lose its sting?

In the bath at night, I wash my skull,
pressing my palm into the meager scalp.
My hair, gone years ago, left but an inch of flesh
between my hands and the immortal bone.
Long after everything that makes me
quirky and unrealized has vanished,
this cap of bone will still survive.
In a coffin most likely, against
some pink sateen.
       Maybe I should say good bye to my too-hard head.

It's flesh I fancy. My middle fingers
warm the empty hollows
of my face, massage my lips.
Oh lost and lingering flesh! Eyes, nose,
cartilage—all like spirit, fade.
I am part of it, my flesh,
my cheeks and eyes and lips are me.
The bone, some distant stranger.

Anne Kaier's essay "Maple Lane" was mentioned on the list of Notables in the 2014 edition of *Best American Essays*. Her new memoir, *Home with Henry*, is out from PS Books. Her essays and poetry appear in *The Gettysburg Review, Alaska Quarterly Review, The Kenyon Review, Referential and Beauty is a Verb: An Anthology of Poetry, Poetics*, and *Disability* which is on the American Library Association Notable Books list for 2012. With a PhD from Harvard University, Kaier teaches at Rosemont College and Arcadia University. She lives in Center City Philadelphia. More at www.annekaier.com.

Down the Back of an Eagle
C.A. Cole

Years ago, her therapist, perched on the opposite couch like a small brown toad in her boxy sweater, a mud-colored shawl thrown over her shoulder, had asked, "What gives you joy?"

"Joy?" Furrows of annoyance creased Monika's forehead before she caught herself and resettled into the non-committal expression she normally reserved for these sessions.

She envisioned joy as frolicking, lifting your arms and skipping with the clouds. Her middle niece danced in giddiness over the smallest thing. But if you were ecstatic over a boy phoning, a movie coming to town, or acceptance at your first choice college all at the same high-pitched screeching intensity, could that be joy or the sign of a deranged mind?

"I'm not a joyous person," she finally said. Only seconds had elapsed. She could have said, "Joy? I'm not a joyous person," without any pause, if only she didn't have mind travels, if she didn't traverse worlds between words.

The therapist raised a bushy eyebrow. "What makes you happy then?"

"Lots of things make me happy, but I've never felt uplifted." Monika raised her palms heavenward as if she were at a revival meeting. "I've never felt the need to shout and exclaim." She lowered her arms. The view over the therapist's shoulder was of dead hollyhock stalks, crinkled leaves clinging to an oak tree, and a striated sky with wisps of snow. "My emotional thermostat must be set low."

They were both in their late thirties. The therapist didn't have children, hadn't had a steady relationship, only housemates, yet her shifting on the vinyl couch, and the dazzle in her umber eyes implied she possessed knowledge Monika lacked.

The summer after she quit therapy, Monika's friend Helen visited. After supper the two of them settled on the back porch, the Colorado sun etching soft fuzz halos around their faces. Monika wanted to grab a pencil to sketch the shadows on her friend's cheek, but instead she asked, "What's joyous for you?" and idly memorized the play of light under Helen's chin.

"Life events," Helen said, rocking in the rusty glider. "Watching my nieces go off to school. Helping Mom navigate one more day. My sisters getting married."

What Monika remembered from her own wedding was whispering in Tom's ear over the screams of an uninvited toddler and the shouting of her father and uncles, "Let's get out of here."

Tom had snugged an arm around her waist as she clutched a handful of her cotton skirt. They'd lowered their heads and squeezed through the drunken crowd to the waiting car. Multicolored paper shreds twirled in the air, red and blue dandruff mottling her dark hair. She scanned the fringes of the crowd hoping for one last glimpse of Dane before she left upstate New York but knew the ghostly outline against the brick church was the sequelae of her neurons misfiring.

She'd worked a factory job to help Tom through veterinary school. She had evenings free, which might have been why Tom surprised her with a needlepoint kit. That had annoyed her, as if he didn't think reading all night was a worthwhile activity, but she discovered the monotony of canvas work soothed her. As she stuck thick red and green and purple threads through taut cloth, she whispered her mantra over and over, *Dane, Dane, Dane Miller, where are you? Why am I still crazy about you?*

"Monika?" Tom called, coming in from late night study sessions.

She refocused, blaming him for her betrayal because wouldn't she have been safer reading, caught up in someone else's drama and not creating her own? That was what she'd been doing—still was—making Dane into a drama to excite her mundane existence. She knew that but couldn't control the chimerical shiver from his lips on her neck.

For years she hadn't done any artwork (switching colors in needlepoint kits hardly counted as creative) other than doodling in staff meetings, making loops and circles. Her supervisor glared, as if doodling took effort and concentration she was misplacing. "Look," she told Helen after one meeting, "the doodling helps me listen."

"Ridiculous," Helen had said. "You have to watch the speaker to concentrate."

Monika exhaled a large volume of air. "Helen, I keep telling you, we're different. I don't need to read lips. I'm not you. You're not me."

"Thank goodness," Helen said and slapped down the stack of papers she was carrying. "Are you and Tom coming over this weekend?"

Because no matter how much of a problem she and Helen had communicating at work, they fared well on weekends while weeding the garden in back of Monika's house. Helen took the tomatoes and cabbage, raspberries and beans to process, returning half to Monika. Every spring, pea shoots poking through the barely thawed earth gave Monika momentary delight, but the dread of encroaching bindweed stifled any joy.

When Helen moved to Nebraska to be near her aging mother, the minuscule research office she had founded floundered. Monika was out of a job, seeing the therapist, and moping over the loss of her closest friend.

While searching for a new job, she stumbled upon picture marquetry.

Wood grain in overlapping rings like ripples in a river, a placid lake in the evening sun, whorls of an angry sky, mahogany shadows, or a birch moon almost ignited nascent joy. She sketched redbud trees, the barn and white grass. Back then she wasn't about to admit to the therapist–dressed for spring in bright green as if she'd transmogrified into a frog—that this time—consuming passion almost, almost corresponded to joy. The results of drawing, tracing, cutting, fitting, and fretting were never what she envisioned, plummeting her into near despair. Instead of exploring that with her therapist, she started working at the library and quit counseling before she couldn't contain the secret of Dane one session longer.

The first time she sold an intricate magnolia, spalted maple, and lacewood picture of her own design she'd been gratified, but that heart-thumping happiness, that wasn't exactly joy, either. The headiness of the sale had been tempered by the many easier pieces she'd sold previously, pieces stuck together with the stock parts of others' design. Compounding that were all her squandered squares of expensive veneer.

Well into her forties, Monika contemplated joy at odd intervals: when she was walking the dog, skiing through fresh powder, or watching her niece score the winning soccer goal. Was that joy? It was fun and momentarily electrifying, but joyous?

Would she ever know joy? It was a reasonable question, Monika thought, ten, fifteen years after those therapy sessions. She'd lie awake, the hours grinding toward morning, thinking. Was it like childbirth? Something she'd never actually desired, but then, if she hadn't experienced it, how did she know with any degree of certainty she didn't desire it? Tom often had a special glow when he returned from calving or foaling, kidding goats. She'd never even witnessed the birth of puppies. All their dogs, like their current Lab, Hamlet, had been neutered males.

Or sex? Was sex joyous? Exciting, exhilarating, exhausting, but joyous? Maybe, maybe with the right person under the right circumstances. Having been married to the same man for approaching three decades, maybe she'd missed that opportunity. Maybe it had happened so long ago, she'd forgotten.

Maybe, maybe, the moment she spied Dane at the recent reunion, her thirtieth, she'd experienced a slight uptick in happiness. But he'd hardly done more than say hello, pressing his business card into her hand. His email address was scribbled at the bottom. Not much of a joyous cross-country trek if the most she could take back was the memory of that momentary mingling of their fingers in the hall outside the restroom. Anti-joy, the absence of what could be, the never-was.

She waited a week before she emailed. At first the correspondence moved at the glacial rate of the post office, a message every week at best. Around the holidays it picked up as he complained about the celebrations, the meals he was eating alone because his grown daughter was at her mother's.

Their partial reconnection hardly produced joy. It was a form of happiness—a letting out of breath, a slowing of her heartbeat—although the days when there was no message made her feel as pedestrian as plywood. The overall sum was not bliss.

Even imagining Dane kissing her neck, running his lips lightly over the ridges of her ears, even that slightly salacious daydream was tinged with guilt, worry about what Tom would think, what Tom would feel; it didn't seem possible joy could accumulate at another's expense. Maybe joy was an emotion she would never experience, not with Dane, not with Tom, not with herself.

Wood scents—white oak redolent of whiskey, padauk's hint of cinnamon, the crushed flower of black walnut—steeped in the dusty corners of her family room. For hours, the dog at her feet, she sorted through her box of veneer planks, selecting the perfect grain for background, a snowy mountain peak, or the petals of a purple trillium.

She was working on a large picture of snow clinging to the north-facing ripples in the field out the back door, fitting pine slivers to represent white grass next to darker fine lines of mahogany to provide shadow, when Dane sent her the email about the eagle.

Guess what I saw this weekend, flying over the river, its wingspan almost as wide as the Susquehanna? She knew he was exaggerating; rivers in the east were much wider than those in Colorado, and the only way the wingspan would appear that expansive would be if you were seated behind the bird's wings, sighting down its back. *A bald eagle!!!! I've never seen one in New York before, not in any of my almost fifty years. Fifty years and a first, a bird so majestic, and then later, five minutes later, another. Flying in the opposite direction. Two! It made my weekend. My week, my month. But then, maybe you see them all the time out west.*

She might have seen one, once, soaring out in the field behind the house, swooping to catch a mouse. That had been when they first moved to the country and there weren't faux bungalows springing up behind every cornstalk, the road had been gravel, and the traffic sparse. She wrote back yes, she had seen one, but not for years, and when Tom arrived home—on time for once, no last minute equine legs to splint, no frothing farm dogs to put down—she checked with him, and he affirmed there had been an eagle in the field one whole summer.

"Don't know what happened to it, or where its mate was," he said, shaking his head as he pulled off his watch cap. He'd been out in a barnyard all afternoon and smelled like dung and sour milk. He stripped, and she gathered his clothes to shove in the washer.

"Its mate?"

"Bald eagles mate for life," he told her and kissed the top of her head where her part split. "Like swans."

As soon as she heard the shower, she wrote back to Dane, suggesting maybe the two eagles he saw were a pair, and he jotted back he hoped so. The quickness of his response, as well as the idea that even if he didn't have a true mate of his own, even if it was an ideal he'd never achieve, he romanticized the concept of mating for life, sent shivers up her back.

"So I hear people are spotting eagles in New York," she told Tom when he emerged for dinner, drying his hair with a towel. "I don't remember ever seeing one."

"Bald eagles? In New York?" He folded his damp towel and poured the wine she'd opened earlier to breathe. "They aren't endangered anymore, just threatened. That may change later this year."

She sliced the pot roast with the stabbing motion she used around curves when hand cutting veneers. She wasn't likely to remember any bird, not unless someone pointed out the national symbol was a rare sight. Tom told her eagles often nested in the same spot for three years, and some nests had been weighed at two thousand pounds.

"There's a nest in Philadelphia. The first in two hundred years. The City of Liberty." He grinned as if that thought alone produced joy.

"Maybe I should do a picture with an eagle," she said, mentally running through her inventory of wood. She'd need something dark like wenge, and light, maybe pearwood. Usually she didn't like to do birds. They ended up looking like a pattern rather than her own unique, artistic rendering. She could design a plaque, maybe sketch one of her beloved redbud trees in the foreground, and send it to Dane. Tom would never know.

That night, the wind howled through the oak branches outside their window. Dane's dawn would have already settled over the freshly greening earth, the sun lighting the tips of trees, storm clouds yellowing in the morning light. These days he often wrote her a note before his day began. She imagined him clutching a mug of weak coffee, sliding into a grimy chair at his work desk, his long hair, the color of pecan husks, tousled. She liked that he wrote her in the morning; that way she didn't have to spend the day worrying if there would be a missive from him. This way her hopes of a letter in which he spilled his blood, told her he'd been thinking of her all night, too, were dashed early and she could get on with her day.

She wished, damn it, she wasn't such an insufferable romantic; she knew Dane wasn't as enamored of her as she was of him. Never had been. Might never be, and therefore a relationship with him wasn't going to lead to joy, either.

That morning there was nothing. She had the day off, wasn't scheduled to work until the next evening, leaving hours to focus on the absence of communication. She made biscuits and eggs for Tom's breakfast, kissed his bristly cheek goodbye, grabbed a sketchbook and the ball thrower for the dog. Hamlet jumped at her in excitement, skittered across the floor, yowling, until she held the back door open. She passed under the still dormant redbuds on the path from the house to the barn, turned down the slope to the lake. Hamlet yipped, raced to the water's edge, and jumped in, thrashing in impatience.

"Just wait," she yelled. He bounded back to shore, lifting his paws in a prance. As soon as she was close, she launched the ball and he flew after it, whining in joy, belly-flopping into the icy water, and swimming toward the bobbing green speck.

From the shore, the roof of the hired hand's house on the next property was visible. Only in the last year had it been repainted and rented. The older woman who moved in was a cellist. Monika would sneak through the white grass, down along the irrigation ditch and up to the porch to listen as she practiced. The music quivered as if each note were outlined in the morning air. Monika held her breath so nothing interfered with the sound, pure and ebullient. *If only I had some musical talent*, she had thought. Listening to CDs was as close as she came, the soaring of *A Lark Ascending*, the violin's note teetering out of audible range.

Everyone else had their road to joy—a tossed ball for the dog, Helen's involvement with her relatives' lives, Dane's enchantment with wildlife. One of the women at work patted the last book she shelved every day as if she perceived joy in a job well done, a job completed.

To the south a vee of Canada geese dotted the sky, something she could evoke in wood, maybe purple-heart or teak above a bocote lake. They dropped, cannon ball abdomens aiming toward the far end of her lake. She shaded her eyes as they descended, wings cupping the air as they hung, skydivers beneath blooming parachutes.

The shoreline meandered like a thin string of gray pearls. She launched the ball again, and as Hamlet gave chase, the geese closest to shore scrabbled across the choppy surface, their beaks stabbing toward the compass points as they took flight. Hamlet shook himself, dropped the ball at her feet, spattering water on her paper.

Long before the dog was exhausted, she was chilled and ready to trace her new picture. She scooped up the ball and led Hamlet under the redbuds. She sighted through the black branches, imagining the sky as burled myrtle, the branches mahogany. Soon buds would cling in small pink bunches to the bare bark, then open in fuchsia and magenta profusion along the arms, followed by tiny, valentine leaves, and later by clusters of rustling seeds.

She envisioned an eagle soaring, a green heart-shaped leaf in the foreground. In the bright morning air she could hear notes from the neighbor's instrument. It wasn't hard to imagine the cellist raising her bow from the strings and slowly, slowly opening her eyes, coming back to earth after having flown in joy, contentment, lucid rapture.

Against a redbud's barren black branch was the earliest sliver of pink, the bud's nascent softness a contrast to the morning chill. For a moment, for the final second of the cello's lingering note, Monika was ungrounded, then flew as if she were on the back of a bird, winging through the cloudless sky.

C.A. Cole (a.k.a. Catherine Cole Janonis) first published poetry in journals such as *Kalliope* and *Voices International* in the 80s. Her first short story was included in *Modern Short Stories*, published in 1988. Recently, most of her publications have come via flash fiction journals and magazines, including *Smokelong Quarterly*, *Hermeneutic Chaos*, and *Vine Leaves*. C.A. Cole currently lives in Colorado.

Men Kissing
J.C. Todd

Men kissing, men kissing men in a movie,
women kissing, kissing women in the next,
then men kissing women, women, men,

lips swelling into sexual pout,
tongues like petals in storm whorling
on a screen in the basement

of the Methodist Church. Not porn, not instruction
but an ancient lesson—adoration,
how the mouth without words is made holy.

In the diner after the movies, men kissing,
a blonde and a redhead. Over rhubarb pie and coffee
I'm imagining the redhead kissing me.

It's good, as good as any lover,
lips so full I want to gloss them with crimson,
signaling to ruin, Pass over here.

In the shiny metal wall, I glimpse a smeary face,
my own, blurred enough it could be my brother's
leaning toward our father, ready for a bedtime kiss.

My brother, little, kissing our father,
my brother, grown, kissing our father.
Every night of the life they lived together,

Father leaning back in the rocker, tilting his head,
his mouth toward his son, Son leaning down,
thin lips pursed, his nose, so like Mother's,

brushing Father's nose, his stubbled chin
brushing Father's stubbled chin,
the two of them, homophobic and affectionate,

saying goodnight with a kiss as soft
as the first kiss of the men in the movie, the men
in the diner, soft as kisses I have given or received.

J. C. Todd is author of *What Space This Body* (Wind 2008), *Nightshade* and *Entering Pisces*, and *FUBAR*, a limited edition artist book designed by MaryAnn Miller, forthcoming from Lucia Press, 2016. Poems have appeared in *The Paris Review*, *APR*, *Virginia Quarterly Review*, and other journals. A 2014 Pew Fellow in the Arts, Todd holds a Pennsylvania Council on the Arts fellowship, two Leeway Foundation poetry awards, and scholarships to the Baltic Center for Writers and Translators and Kunsterhaus, Schloss Wiepersdorf. A 2015 Fellow of the Virginia Center for the Creative Arts and The Hambidge Center for 2016, she is a Fellow at Ragdale and the Pew Fellow at Ucross. She is faculty member in Creative Writing at Bryn Mawr College and the MFA Program at Rosemont College.

Leaving
Rachael Pastan

When Pauline was ten years old, her parents sent her to riding camp. What a month that was! The sun beating down all day on the horse's manes, the dust rising from the paths, the smell of girls sleeping six to a room. They made you shower on Sundays, but otherwise, as long as you did your chores, they left you alone. You could wear the same jeans every day, the same underwear every day. Brushing and feeding, shining and mucking out. The horses were the important thing.

And when it was over, her father came to get her in his convertible. "There have been some changes," he said. She was thinking of herself, the changes in her. She was taller, stronger, her hair bleached blond by the sun, and she seemed to have learned some things, though she couldn't put into words what they were. So she didn't pick up on his tone until he said, "Your mother and I." Then she had looked up, her heart galloping like a horse itself in her chest.

It wasn't just that her mother was gone; it was that someone new had moved in. And it wasn't just that. It was that Leon, who her father played squash with sometimes, had moved in. Pauline was ten years old; what did she know? What could she understand or guess?

She remembers the first time she saw them kissing, in the kitchen late one night when she came down for a drink of water. And she'd thought, So that's it! How much more settled she felt knowing there was some sense to things, that the world was not just chaos.

Lately, though, it seems like chaos all over again. She is on the train, on her way to see an apartment in the city: one bedroom, high ceilings, river views. For weeks she has been reading the real estate ads in secret, as though they were porn. Not that James would have suspected anything. He always takes her at face value, which is the trouble.

Out the window the trees are getting ready to leaf. Their buds are red and thick against the sky. Why red when the leaves themselves will be green? She doesn't know. Here she is in the full green blossom of her life, and all the things she'll never know buzz past her like bees. The train passes behind industrial buildings, hillsides covered in trash, yellow cranes waiting to lift tons of steel.

James loves her. James with his sturdy body and his wide mouth, his smile, his soft brown hair flecked with the first gray—loves her. He has gone gray loving her. Like her mother, Pauline went gray early. She has been dyeing her hair for years.

Like her mother. Like her father. Can't you ever break free, like a horse on a summer day, galloping? Can't you be borne along on muscle and grace so far and fast that you lose yourself, that you become sun and sky, become movement itself?

In the new apartment, perched on the edge of the river, she'll forget to shower. She'll leave her dirty laundry on the floor, leave the telephone off the hook, leave her windows open as rain clouds gather. She'll lean out the open window as far as she can go and feel on her naked skin the cold kiss of the first drop of water.

Rachel Pastan is the author of the novels *Alena*, *Lady of the Snakes*, and *This Side of Married*. Her short fiction has appeared in *The Georgia Review*, *Mademoiselle*, *The Threepenny Review*, *Prairie Schooner*, *The Virginia Quarterly Review*, and many other places. Pastan is a member of the Core Faculty in Fiction at the Bennington Writing Seminars MFA program and lives outside of Philadelphia.

Bent and Blue

C.J. Spataro

Blue's real name is Bluebelle, if you can believe it, and Bent—his real name is Gerald Bentmeier, but everybody, including me, has always just called them Bent and Blue. I've known Blue longer—the two of us were neighbors of a sort growing up in Twin Lake. Not that Twin Lake isn't much more than a zip code with a stop light. And it ain't Twin Lakes, although it seems like it should be, it ain't. There's one lake with a strip a land down the middle, so it's Twin Lake. I know, it don't make no sense to me either.

My dad works for the county Sheriff's department and Blue's dad owns a little farm and works at a bait and tackle store in town. I never could quite figure out how they paid for everything, but somehow they managed. Her mom was one of them moms that made everything by hand and shopped at the Salvation Army. I'd help Blue milk their cow once in a while. My mom never did want me to drink the milk over there because it wasn't pasteurized. She said it was unsanitary. I drank it anyway. Blue never was sick much, so I figured it couldn't hurt me any. I liked the way it tasted when it was super cold, all creamy and delicious, but truth be told it did smell a little like the inside of a barn.

Blue's parents was really strict, though, so I didn't go over as much as I would have liked to, but she had a horse, and what kid can resist a horse? One day, we come back from riding a little late and Mr. Overton took off his belt and beat her right in front of me. It felt like Blue was looking straight through me as he whipped her, her eyes red and watery, but she didn't cry. I think if she could a killed her dad right then and there, she might have. I didn't know what to do, so I stood off to the side of the barn with my mouth shut and my hands in my pockets till he was done.

Blue and me went to Twin Lake elementary then rode the bus to the junior high together. That's where we met Bent. Technically, I seen Bent first. He was in my homeroom, sitting right in front of me. Gerald Bentmeier, Laurie Crakowski, Sally Denton, Mike Erhlich. That was our row. Bent had a ponytail, which made him a stand out right from the beginning, and it wasn't some stupid trailer park mullet either. His hair was long, front and back. Long, black, and shiny. He kept his hair clean, I'll say that for him, even when things got real bad—and boy it don't get no worse—but his hair was always beautiful.

By the time we was in high school, Mike E. and I was dating steady and Bent and Blue was practically engaged. Them two had some grand ideas. I guess we all did. Bent wanted to be a graphic artist and design album covers.

That kid could really draw, too. He was always doodling, always coming up with something fantastical. He drew a picture a me once, in English class, on a piece a notebook paper. My face is sideways, profile I guess, and my hair is streaming out behind me, and if you look real close you can see flowers and horses and trees and rabbits all hidden in the folds of my hair. I still have that picture; I have it framed and hanging on my wall.

Blue got pregnant our senior year and she was actually pretty happy about it. I'm sure Mr. Overton gave her a good beating the day she told her parents, but what could they do? They was way too religious to let her get an abortion—not that she would have wanted one in a million years anyway. Bent was a different story. He had plans. He wanted to go to community college then maybe even go away to school. I don't think he ever really thought that him and Blue would last past high school, but the baby changed all that.

The Saturday after graduation, me and Mike E. stood up for them at their wedding. Blue's parents didn't have no money, but Bent's parents had a cottage up north on Lake Michigan, where they had the ceremony. Blue's parents almost didn't come because they weren't getting married in a church, but then Blue's dad said, "What difference does it make? She's already pregnant." And her mom agreed.

The ceremony was beautiful. They got married just as the bright orange sunset slipped down behind the horizon, making the sky all pink and purple. It was a warm day for June and I got to wear a really pretty dress that Blue picked out for me. It was lime green chiffon and I wore flowers in my hair. Mike E. looked handsome, too; he had a matching lime green cummerbund and bow tie.

Bent's parents were pretty cool about the whole thing. Blue and him were going to live with them for a while until he had enough money saved up for a house. His dad even got him a job at the big foundry just south of Whitehall where he was a foreman. Them foundry jobs was hard to come by and Bent knew he was lucky to get it, even if his dad was the foreman, but still, it wasn't what he wanted to do. Blue was just happy to get out of Twin Lake and off the farm.

I got a job at the Meijer's in North Muskegon that summer, as a cashier, and a couple of months after her baby was born, Blue got a job there too. Bent's mom looked after little Tiffany while Blue was at work and seemed happy to take care of her grandbaby. Bent didn't seem too happy, though. At least that's what I thought. Something was off, even back then, but whenever I'd ask Blue about it she'd tell me he was just tired. Working overtime and taking care of the baby was a lot for a guy to handle.

"You don't know how lucky you are, Blue," I said to her as we was driving to work one day. She looked at me funny, kind a wrinkled up her nose.

"Seriously, Blue. Lots a people would a just cut you guys loose. Bent's parents are great."

She shrugged. "I just can't wait to have a house of our own. With both me and Jerry working, we should have enough money saved up in no time."

After they got married, Blue started calling Bent "Jerry." That was the name his parents called him. Jerry. It just didn't suit him, and that's all I can say about that.

That day always sticks in my mind, I guess, because of what happened later. I was standing at my cash register, ringing people up, my mind wandering, thinking about how at nineteen Blue was going to have a real home and family all her own, that things really were looking good for her. When it was time for us to go on break she grabbed me by the hand and pulled me all the way through the grocery and sporting goods and back into the pharmacy.

"What are we doing back here?" Then I saw where we were standing. In front of the pregnancy tests. My stomach did a flip-flop. I knew I wasn't pregnant. I may not be the smartest girl in the world, but I know enough to take the pill. Blue stood there, smiling at me.

"Are you sure?" I shoved my hands into my apron and stared at my sneakers.

"Well, I'll have to go to the doctor, of course, but I'm pretty sure." She sounded happy.

"I didn't think you could get pregnant this close after having a baby." I couldn't look at her. How could she be happy about this?

"It's gonna be okay, Laurie, don't worry. Jerry wants to have a big family. We talk about it all the time."

I swallowed hard. "Blue, I don't think Bent wanted to have two kids before he was twenty."

She wrapped her arms around herself and stared at me, that same hard expression she had that day her dad whipped her. "You don't know him the way I do, Laurie. He loves Tiffany and he'll love this baby too."

What could I do? She was my best friend—I had to be happy for her.

"Congratulations," I said and gave her a big hug. "I'm sure you're right."

It wasn't too long after Amber was born that Blue got pregnant again with Jerry, Jr. Bent started working nights at the foundry. The company had just gotten a big government contract and hired a bunch of guys and Mike E. got a job there too. Bent worked the graveyard shift, told Mike E. it was better money and all, but I figured he just couldn't stand being in that house at night with one more kid. J.J.—that's what me and Blue called the baby—

was a sweet one, but that Amber had a pair a lungs on her. Sometimes when I came to visit I could hear her crying inside the house before I even got out of my car. I don't know how Bent ever got any sleep. Mike and me figured that's why he started drinking a little more than he used to. It must a helped him sleep.

Blue and me was in her kitchen, getting ready for Bent's surprise birthday party. They'd moved into their house in Lakewood Club, not too far from the foundry, just before Amber was born. It was a nice, cozy place but a little too isolated for my taste. Blue seemed to love it, said it didn't remind her of the farm at all. She quit her job at Meijer's when she got pregnant with Jerry, Jr. Raising three kids was a full-time job, she said, and she worked hard to make the house nice for all a them.

Blue pulled the cake out of the oven and started whipping up the frosting. One good thing she learned from her mother was how to cook. She could make the best dinners out of practically nothing. I'd bring her groceries sometimes, since I got a discount at Meijer's, and I'd buy her some clothes for the babies too. Tiffany was almost five and getting ready for kindergarten in the fall. She was a pretty little thing, with long dark hair just like Bent and fierce green eyes like Blue. I told her I thought Tiffany was smarter than the both of us put together and Blue agreed.

I fixed me and Blue a drink while Tiffany helped wrap Bent's present, a real nice set of colored pencils with pastels and a big fancy pad of paper. Blue went all the way to Grand Rapids, to some ritzy art store, for it. I remember because I was babysitting that day and Amber was sick.

We had another drink and I helped Blue make dinner. It wasn't nothing fancy, but it was Bent's favorite: fried chicken with potato salad and string beans. Mike E. was coming over, and so were a couple of Bent's friends from the foundry and his parents. I didn't know where Bent was, just that it was his day off and he was out.

By seven o'clock, everyone had been there already for an hour or so and still no sign of Bent. Blue said she wasn't worried but maybe she'd better go ahead and feed the kids. Bent's mom made a few phone calls, but no one seemed to know where he'd gone off to. By nine the kids was in bed and the adults were starving. I never seen people eat so fast in all my life. Blue managed to save a plate for Bent and we didn't touch the birthday cake. The beer was gone by eleven and so was most of the party. Me and Mike E. said we'd go out and take a spin to some of Bent's places, maybe we could find him and bring him home. Blue said she wasn't worried, but I knew what she was thinking. Bent had another girl and was celebrating his birthday with her.

Mike and me got in his Camaro and headed up toward Whitehall. It was early April and starting to get warm during the day, but there were still clumps of dirty snow near the edge of the road and in the woods.

"Relax, Laurie," he said, slipping his favorite Foreigner tape into the deck. "We'll find Bent."

I was not convinced. "Do you know where he is?"

"No I do not," said Mike. "Not for sure, anyway."

I fumbled in my purse for a cigarette. "Do you think he's having an affair?"

Mike laughed. "Come on Laurie, Bent? He don't have the energy for the woman he's got."

I smiled and cracked open the window. "I guess you're right. You think he's just out drinking or something?"

"Between you and me, he's been acting a little weird lately. Last time we went bowling, I caught him mumbling to himself." Mike shook his head. "Something about Jesus and the flames of eternity, but I don't know what he was saying."

"Did you ask him about it?"

"He just looked at me like *I* was the crazy one."

I flicked some ash out the window and watched the spark as it danced along the dark road. "Maybe it's the heat. He's running the smelter now, ain't he?"

"Who knows, Laur, who knows? Bent's always been a little off."

"Is that a nice thing to say about your best friend?" The cigarette turned sour in my mouth and I shoved the butt out the window.

"He ain't my best friend. And it's true, you know it."

Mike swung the car through Whitehall, which is about four times bigger than Twin Lake—meaning it has four stop lights. Nobody was on the street. The Porthole was still open, so we stopped in there and had a quick beer, but no one had seen Bent all night. Mike and me weren't sure where to go next and I'll admit we was a little buzzed by this point. Somehow Mike got it in his head to check out the Lake. I told him he was crazy. It was way too cold to be down on the beach. Bent had probably gone into Muskegon and, if he had, we'd never find him.

"What can it hurt, Laur, it's on our way back to Blue's."

I nodded and got in the car. We decided that, if he was at the beach in the middle of the night, he would probably be down by Duck Lake, which is really a pond that's directly connected to Lake Michigan by a little channel. In the summertime, everyone wants to go there because the water is so shallow. It's a whole lot warmer than Lake Michigan, but if you want to go sailing or something, the big lake is right there. I knew Bent liked it because there were some really great dunes along that part of the beach and he loved to draw them.

As soon as we rounded the bend, we seen Bent's pickup.

"Jesus, he *is* here," Mike said.

The wind was whipping off the Lake and it felt like we might get one of them freak April snowstorms. I pulled my coat tighter around me, wishing I had my ski hat and gloves. Mike grabbed his flashlight from the trunk and set out across the dunes. It didn't take us long to find Bent. He was standing at the top of the dune, arms spread wide, his shirt, shoes, pants, and coat piled in a heap at his feet. His hair was loose and swirled around his head like octopus tentacles. I ain't ashamed to say that I was scared. Even in the dim light we could see that Bent had cut himself and there was blood trickling down his bare arms and chest. Mike was scared too, I could tell. Bent was talking to himself and we couldn't understand what he was saying. I grabbed onto Mike's hand, which he squeezed tight.

"Bent? Bent honey, it's me, Laurie." We stopped a good few yards away from him. My voice felt tiny in the wind coming off the Lake. "Bent, it's Laurie. Why don't you let us drive you home?"

He turned his head, and in the moonlight I could see that he was gone. Bent was now in a very faraway place. Mike backed us up a few paces.

"Laurie, you need to go call your dad. Tell him we need some help."

"I can't leave you here."

"I'll be fine."

Bent had turned away from us now and was staring back out at the water. His mumble was turning into a growl.

Mike shoved his keys into my hand. "Just go," he said. He pushed me a little harder than he intended, I think, and I slid backward down the sand. My stomach felt like it was in my throat as I ran to the car.

I had to go all the way back to Whitehall before I found a phone. By the time I got my dad on the line I was crying pretty good.

"It's Bent," I said. "Dad, he's gone completely crazy. Me and Mike are out by Duck Lake and he's cut himself—" I couldn't finish. My dad took over. Being a cop, he knew exactly what to do. By the time I got back to the lake, there were cops from the county, the township, and the state police all over the place. I waited by the side of the road and tried not to think about how Mike'd been out there all alone with Bent. It wasn't right—none of it. It took four cops, plus Mike, to wrestle Bent to the ground and get the knife out of his hands. My dad put his arm around me as the state troopers drove Bent, handcuffed at the wrists and ankles, to the hospital.

"I seen this a couple a times," he said to me. "I ain't a doctor, but it looks like schizophrenia to me."

Well, my dad was right. Paranoid Schizophrenia with delusions of grandeur. Sounded to me like an English teacher I had in high school. Blue never did appreciate that joke too much, but I had to try and cheer her up somehow. I used to drive her to the state mental hospital in Traverse City where they had Bent locked up. He was real bad off. It took almost four hours to get there, so we didn't go too much at first. Bent didn't even recognize his own parents for a long time, but the doctors kept telling Blue that he would get better once the medication had a chance to take hold. Turns out Blue was waiting to tell Bent about another baby the night he went off the deep end. She never did tell him, only me, and that's because she wanted me to drive her to the abortion clinic in Grand Rapids. Said it was a birthday present she just couldn't afford to give him right now. I think Mrs. Bentmeier knew what was going on, but she didn't say nothing to Blue or me about it. She came over and made cookies with her grandkids while Blue and me were at the clinic. I don't know what was scarier, that silent trip home from G. R. with Blue crying in the front seat of my car or seeing Bent all doped up like a zombie in a straitjacket. Life sure seemed to be taking a turn for the worse.

Bent was in the hospital for almost a year before they let him out. While he was away, me and Mike E. decided to get married. I'd dated a few other guys, but none a them was near as nice as Mike. They made me a head cashier at Meijer's and me and Mike bought a little house not too far from my folks in Twin Lake. Blue went back to work at the Meijer's and Mrs. Bentmeier watched the kids during the day.

Bent wasn't really the same when he come home. He was tired all the time and slept a lot. The doctors said he was doing real good, but it didn't seem like it to me or to Blue. He didn't want to play with the kids, or go fishing, or even draw anymore. Every time I went over to their house he was just sitting in the living room, in his bathrobe, watching TV and drinking beer. Which I'm sure he wasn't supposed to be doing anyway. I felt sorry for him, and Blue too, of course. She was working harder than she ever thought she'd have to, but what could she do? Bent's disability checks would only go so far. Sometimes I'd sit and talk to Bent about art and stuff when Blue was in the kitchen or doing something with the kids. I was taking a class at the community college and could see how much talent Bent had, but he didn't seem too interested. Blue got plenty frustrated with him too, the way he sat around all day doing nothing. Everyone told her she should be patient and the doctors told her he would get better.

And he did, or so it seemed. After a while he perked up some, didn't seem so moody. Him and Mike went out on Mike's boat once or twice. They even took the kids and told everyone they had a grand time. Blue started getting that dreamy look in her eye again, and I told her she better not be thinking about having any more kids. It had been about eighteen months since Bent had his breakdown when he decided he wanted to go back to work. None of us was quite sure that was the right thing, but his dad got him a part-time shift on the smelter, which seemed to suit everybody just fine.

Maybe it was all them chemicals that messed him up in the end, or maybe it was the heat. I guess nobody'll ever really know for sure. He just seemed to be doing so much better that it came as a real shock when Blue found him in the bathroom one night after work. She knew right where to go, because she heard Amber wailing the minute she walked in the door, leastways that's what she told me. The TV was on and so was every light in the house. Up in the bathroom, Bent had lit every candle he could find. J.J. and Tiffany was sitting on the edge of the tub in their underpants, their little hands tied behind their backs, sniffling. Amber was sitting on the toilet lid, and her hands were tied too. Bent had shaved all of their beautiful little heads. Amber's head was nicked and bleeding—that's why she was crying so hard, I guess. He'd shaved J.J.'s eyebrows too. Blue freaked. Bent kept saying that the kids needed to be purified, first by water and then by fire, or they wouldn't be saved. Blue called the cops and had him arrested.

Turns out Bent had seemed so much better 'cause he'd stopped taking his medicine. Well, he seemed better until he snapped, that is. I don't mean to be flip, but I don't know how else to put it. They locked him up in the psych ward of the county hospital this time and forced the medication on him. Blue begged me to go with her to see him, for moral support. I hated seeing him like that, but I had to be there for Blue. She was my best friend.

Bent was in a locked ward, and when they brought him in to see me and Blue, it looked to me like he'd been crying. He had on a floppy hospital gown and a dingy bathrobe. His feet must a been freezing, 'cause all he had on them was flip-flops. He sat down across from us and stared hard at Blue. It was a long time before anybody said anything.

"Blue, I'm real sorry. I didn't hurt the kids, did I?" He did look sorry, I thought, but I knew Blue had made up her mind.

"It don't matter, Jerry." Blue had her hands in her lap. I don't think she could quite bring herself to look at Bent fully in the eye.

"What do you mean it don't matter?" He leaned forward a little. His neck was red.

"It means you can't come home," she said, shaking her head. "I made up my mind."

"Well, don't I get a say? It's my house too," he said. He stood up. The orderly came over and placed his hand on Bent's shoulder and he sat back down.

"That's true. If you want me and the kids to move out, we'll find a place, but we're done."

Bent's head swiveled in my direction. "You put her up to this didn't you, Laurie?"

"Me?" I sat back a little in my chair. "Nobody can put Blue up to anything, you ought to know that by now, Bent."

"Don't call me that!" He put his head down and pounded his fists on the table. "Don't call me that. Don't call me that."

Blue and I both shoved our chairs back at the same time, we was so startled.

"You're going to have to settle down, Mr. Bentmeier, or your visit will be over."

Bent's eyes were red and kind a bulging out of his head a little, like he was trying not to cry. I didn't want to upset him. I was sorry and I said so. He sat up straight and nodded to the orderly. Me and Blue kind a relaxed a little bit, but we was scared. Sorry and scared.

"I'll call you Jerry, if you want me to," I said finally.

"It's the damn medicine. It makes me so groggy. I can't draw, I can't do nothing. I feel like I got a wet bag of leaves over my head."

Me and Blue looked at him, not knowing what to say.

"Why can't I just be normal again?"

Blue shook her head and reached for my hand. I could tell she wanted to cry real bad, but she was trying to hold it together for Bent.

Bent wasn't in the hospital for too long this time. Once they got him back on his pills they let him out. While he was away, Blue had filed for divorce and sole custody of the kids. Mr. and Mrs. Bentmeier understood, but they wasn't too happy about the whole situation. Bent moved into their basement and could only see the kids when he was at his parent's house. The kids really was afraid of him at first, which was totally understandable under the circumstances. I was a little afraid of him too.

Bent's mom refused to believe that anything was really wrong with Bent. She cooked his meals and pampered him like a little kid. She would have made his bed and dusted his room, too, except Bent went out and got a padlock for the door, saying a man had a right to his privacy. She acted like the whole problem was with Blue, that Blue had never been a good wife— that Blue'd never been good for Bent at all. That may have been true. I've thought, once or twice in my secret heart, that maybe Blue wasn't no good for Bent, that she held him back by having all those kids. He never really had a chance to find his true self. But if I'm honest, I know that ain't totally right. It wasn't Blue's fault Bent got sick and shaved his kids' heads.

Things seemed to settle down for a while. Blue started seeing Mike E.'s cousin Fred, a real cute college boy from Grand Haven. Bent would call her once in a while, in the middle of the night, she said, and then hang up. Mike said he was still working at the foundry, but only part-time, and that everyone there kind a kept their distance, even though Bent's dad was the foreman. I thought about Bent a lot in those days, but I never did go see him. I'm not really sure why.

It was around Christmastime when Fred said he wanted to take Blue skiing up at Boyne. Blue asked me to watch the kids for her, but Bent's mom wanted to take them for the holiday. Mrs. Bentmeier didn't much approve of Fred and Blue, or of me, even though I was finally expecting my first one later that year. Blue was a little nervous about leaving the kids overnight, but she trusted Mr. and Mrs. Bentmeier. She knew they loved their grandkids, even if they had no use for her anymore.

Blue kissed them kids good-bye on a snowy morning, the day after Christmas, and left with Fred to go skiing. How it all happened, I don't think we'll ever know for sure. Turns out Bent'd been flushing his pills down the toilet, and not even his mother knew it. You can't look at that woman now, I'll tell you what. She aged twenty years in a day, can't look nobody in the eye when she passes them on the street.

Seems Bent told his parents that he needed to go out for a bit, pick up some stuff at the grocery, maybe get a few supplies at the new art store down in Muskegon. They didn't think nothing of it. Bent spent a lot of time drawing. They all thought it was therapeutic. His parents swear up and down that he was fine when he left the house, but I don't believe them. I don't believe them one bit. It'd been quite a while since the hair-shaving incident and the kids, like kids do, had forgotten all about it. Mrs. Bentmeier had them all wound up on Christmas candy and cookies and Amber, as usual, was sick. Tiffany and J.J. decided they wanted to go for a ride with their dad, and for some reason everyone thought that would be okay.

Bent strapped them into the backseat of his dad's Ford and drove to the foundry. Mike was working that day with a skeleton crew, because of the holidays and all. They was mostly just cleaning up, working in the front part of the foundry. Mike didn't think nothing was wrong, didn't hear Bent or the kids come in the side door, until they heard the motor on the swing arm to the smelter fire up. As soon as they heard that, they dropped what they was doing, which Mike don't even remember now, and ran to the smelting room.

Mike and his crew found Bent staring into the furnace flames with that same faraway look on his face that he had that night on the dune.

"The children have been purified by fire," Bent said. Mike told me he was smiling and crying at the same time. "They are safe. Nothing can hurt them now. Not even me."

No one ever thought in a million years that Bent could actually hurt his kids, medication or not, but it seems we was all wrong—about everything. Bent had put his kids in the smelter and turned the furnace on. It was all over for them in less than thirty seconds. They had to do tests on the ash left in the bowl to prove what he done, that he hadn't stashed them someplace, or done something else. The whole county was sick about it. Mike couldn't go back to work. He felt responsible, like he could a stopped Bent from doing it, but we all know that ain't true. It's too bad Bent didn't burn himself up instead. It's mean to say something like that, I know, but everybody would a been a lot better off—especially his kids.

My dad told me that when the police searched Bent's room at his parent's house they saw that he'd painted some kind of fantastical mural on the walls. Giant red flames rose from the floor to the ceiling and, according to my dad, intertwined in them flames was all kinds of stuff you couldn't see in the pictures they printed in the paper. There were skeletons and ghosts and saints and all kinds a animals. Dad said that if the whole thing hadn't been so sickening, the mural might have almost been beautiful.

Blue wasn't never the same. The only time she lets Amber out of her sight is when the kid is at school, and even then she picks her up and drops her off every day. I don't really blame her. I hold on to my little one a tighter than I should probably, but I can't help myself.

Michigan don't have the death penalty, but plenty of folks around here sure thought they should a made an exception for Bent. He knew he was dangerous when he didn't take his pills, but he did it anyway—in the eyes of the law that makes him responsible, and I have to say that I agree.

Mike got a job working in a lumber yard as a manager. Doesn't pay as good as at the foundry, but he likes being outside, he says, and away from the smelter. Mikey's about three years old now, and he loves to draw. Mike don't much care for that and hates it when I put the pictures up on the fridge, but I do it anyway. I love Mike and I love our kid. When Mike ain't home, I get out the pastels and paper that Blue gave me after Bent went to prison, and me and Mikey Jr. sit on the floor and draw and draw and draw.

Carla "C.J." Spataro, editorial director *Philadelphia Stories Magazine* and PS Books, is a Pennsylvania Council on the Arts Fellowship recipient for fiction. Her work can be read in *Painted Bride Quarterly*, *Wild River Review*, *XConnect*, *Mason's Road*, *The Baltimore Review*, and other journals. She is the program director of Rosemont College's MFA in Creative Writing and has taught English, journalism, and creative writing courses at a number of Philadelphia area colleges.

Sugar Ants

Miriam N. Kotzin

No matter how many times Carol Lee scrubbed, she looked for the stain whenever she sat at the kitchen table. The cup she hurled had nicked the wall and splattered coffee in a dark starburst with streamers running down into the crack between the wall and baseboard. Three teaspoons of sugar in the coffee invited a persistent infestation of sugar ants.

She hated the heavy diner-style cup, and wasn't sorry to smash it. She hadn't aimed at her husband. She'd intended the cup to whizz by Frank's head, just to get him to look up from his laptop, to talk to her instead of click click clicking, meal after meal.

She imagined the miniscule feet of the sugar ants inaudible on the tile floor, invisible on the fancy granite counter.

The cup, sailing within inches of his ear, failed to get Frank's attention, but he looked up at the sharp sounds of the cup hitting the wall, the china shattering on the floor, and Carol Lee's wordless wail of outrage.

"Something wrong?" His tone was empty of irony.

She was furious with him but more so at herself for reverting to what she thought of as "trash." She was also a bit short of breath. The cup had come closer to hitting him than she'd expected, but he had no way of knowing that.

"Wrong? Do I throw cups at the wall every morning?" At the wall. That ought to make her intentions clear.

Her mother taught her to hate sugar ants when they appeared on the speckled green linoleum tiles, the white Formica counter, the porcelain sink board. They made her mother crazy. Vinegar. Hot water. Ammonia. They always came back. Now they were here.

Before she pushed her chair away from the table, she hadn't decided whether she'd walk right out of the kitchen or clean up. She'd done enough damage. She bent to get the largest shards and dropped them in the trash. She grabbed five or six paper towels. Squatting, she wiped the coffee from the floor and used the same paper towel to pick up the smaller pieces within a three-foot radius. She'd wet mop the sticky floor later.

"Need help with that?"

Good Lord above, while she was down there cleaning up the slivers of china, Frank was clicking away on those computer keys.

"What will it take, Frank?" She spoke from a crouching position, balanced on the fingertips of her free hand. Would he think she's cowering, or ready to spring? White shards were under Frank's chair, too. She'd get those later.

"I am not tactful like you," she said, pronouncing each syllable as though she were reading from a formal script. She'd screamed these words at him many times in her imagination. Never before, however, had she even thought of hurling something at, that is, past him.

"You can be," he said. "You're the soul of tact when you think it counts."

Throwing cups, well, that was nothing to do with tact. That was a whole other category of rhetoric, but he would never say so. Instead he accused her of undervaluing him. Carol Lee's face burned. Without looking in a mirror, she knew each cheek had a red spot like clown's. It happened whenever she was humiliated.

How small would she have to be so she could hear them? Click click click. They marched from behind the baseboard and the dried sweet coffee that would be there forever.

That was what this was about. Undervaluing. "Thank you," she said.

She wouldn't say she was sorry until she meant it.

"I won't be home for dinner tonight," she said, surprising herself with her declaration. Where would she go?

He raised an eyebrow, then clicked at the computer. "I don't see anything here."

"Not everything's on the computer," she said. She stood over him. She held the wadded up paper towel with the slivers of the smashed cup. The computer was open, vulnerable. Screen. Keyboard.

He looked at her straight on, his face as blank as a dark screen, and clicked the computer closed. He'd slide it into its case and take it with him when he left. "I'll fend for myself, then."

She tossed the damp paper into the garbage. What was the rule for broken china? How small did the piece have to be before it disqualified itself from the recycling bin?

She'd start on the wall when he left. She couldn't let the stain set in. She'd have to do the whole wall. You can't clean just a small spot. Ever. She'd learned that early on in their marriage, getting a bit of jam off the wall. That had been an accident, Frank had tossed a jammy napkin into the trash and missed. A wall isn't a backboard.

Had she been tactful then? She couldn't remember what she'd said, only the hours of scrubbing.

"I won't be late," she said, "not too late." She could always say she had a change of plans and be home, fix dinner, hope he'd be there.

He'd be too tactful to quiz her. Or too indifferent. He wore his good manners like a mask.

She clenched her teeth. She'd have to remember not to go barefoot. No matter how she tried to clean up, weeks after an accident some sliver of glass showed up underfoot. She had cuts to prove it. She'd been raised to believe that only a slattern goes barefoot in the house. She went barefoot anyway.

Sweet coffee behind the baseboard? She'd set out a permanent buffet. Frank, she thought, would ignore sugar ants even in his own home, like it's bad manners to attend to vermin. One day it would get so he'd have to pay them some mind; by then the damage would be irremediable.

More than one cup had shattered on this floor. Anything they dropped broke. Tile floors were unforgiving too.

Miriam N. Kotzin is Professor of English at Drexel University where she teaches creative writing and literature. She is author of a novel, *The Real Deal* (Brick House Press 2012), a collection of flash fiction, *Just Desserts* (Star Cloud Press 2010) and four collections of poetry, *The Body's Bride* (David Robert Books 2013), *Reclaiming the Dead* (New American Press 2008), *Weights & Measures* (Star Cloud Press 2009), and *Taking Stock* (Star Cloud Press 2010). Her poetry received six nominations for a Pushcart Prize. Her poetry has been published in or is forthcoming in *Shenandoah, Boulevard, The Tower Journal, Eclectica, Offcourse,* and *Valparaiso Poetry Review,* among others. She is founding editor of *Per Contra* and has been a contributing editor of *Boulevard* since its inception.

The White Woman Will Eat You
Laura Zimmer-Tamakoshi

{The island of New Guinea, the 'land of the unexpected,' was the last ma-jor landmass to be explored by Europeans. Located in the South Pacific, New Guinea is a place of great contrasts and diversity. Coral islands, mangrove swamps, vast river systems, dense rainforests, and alpine tundra on the highest mountains are home to immense bio- and cultural diversity. Divided among Dutch, German and British colonizers in 1884, New Guinea is now divided roughly in half. The western half consists of two provinces of Indonesia (Papua and West Papua) while the eastern part forms the mainland of Papua New Guinea, which has been an independent country since 1975. New Guinea's indigenous peoples have long attracted anthropologists such as Margaret Mead (1901-1978). Mead delighted in New Guinea's rich cultural diversity, using it to demonstrate that things such as gender relations and 'childhood' are as much culturally as biologically determined. I chose Papua New Guinea as my field site (1982 to the present) to study the effects of development and income inequalities in a society that still requires reciprocity of its members in order for them to achieve respectable 'adulthood' and to hold onto valuable land rights. The experience I share here reveals how the anthropologist is as much an 'other' in what to her is a strange land as her chosen 'others' are to her.}

Only little Willie would let me hold him. Round-faced with short, chub-by legs and a full belly, Willie tolerated my cheek-squeezing and the occa-sional hoisting onto my hip to walk around Yandera village, when his moth-er was playing cards or his young babysitters were playing tag or marbles. Only little Willie was unafraid of the white *misis*,* while other toddlers and young children screamed if I came near them. It was, of course, partly the fault of their mothers and older sisters, who would whisper – loud enough for me to hear –

"The white woman will eat you!" or "She's a ghost and will steal you away to America." The children would then shake and cry as they shrank be-hind their mother's backs, a few wetting themselves in terror. Willie, with his mother's large brown eyes and confidence, was unperturbed, his mother laughing at my annoyance with the other women and their teasing, and little Willie digging in my *bilum*ized* to see if there were any crackers or other goodies to eat.

Willie's mother was not afraid of anything, or not much. When I first arrived in the remote mountain village, Margaret quickly befriended me. Many women were reticent and a few standoffish. Big-hearted Margaret was always there, however, when I needed an explanation about some unfamiliar custom or a shoulder to cry on when I thought of the distance between Papua New Guinea and my homeland and family. She never asked for money or stared at me as if I were a revenant nun or ancestor come back to dispense charity or secrets about the white men's road to wealth. No, Margaret was friendly and easy-going, a woman who viewed the world with clear eyes and the candor of someone content to follow the middle road. Margaret had grown up listening to stories told by her parents and grandparents about how, when the first white missionaries visited the Gende in 1932, many villagers believed them to be ghosts and evil spirits. Some ran away in fear, a few – Margaret chuckled – "pissing and shitting themselves." A quick study, Margaret ventured into the white men's towns unafraid when she and her husband Raphael were young and Papua New Guinea was still under Australian rule.

In that first year I lived in Yandera – in 1982 and 1983 – I learned much from Margaret. Disdaining the rocky path of local politics in favor of minding their own business and being good neighbors, she and her husband worked hard together to raise their many children and repay clan elders the large bride price they gave for sturdy Margaret and the generous rights to garden land they passed on to Raphael. They also dutifully supported Raphael's older clan brother Ruge's political ambitions to become one of Yandera's most powerful Big Men, at the same time supporting other village leaders. Sitting comfortably beside Raphael during public card games or while eating meals with their children, exchanging tender and unabashed glances with him during public events, and spending more time away from the village in their gardens than most couples, Margaret and her husband made me question the anthropological truism that sexual antagonism is a universal cultural trait throughout Papua New Guinea highland societies.

Level-headed Margaret was also the first person in the Tundega clan half of the village to express her opinion – privately to me – that Ruge's wife Elizabeth had accidentally set fire to her own house on the morning of the big *singing**. "Elizabeth and Ruge are wrong to blame the fire on Toby's brother. He was helping his mother in her garden and was far from the village when the fire started. I saw Elizabeth go into her house with a lit cigarette and come out without it." That Elizabeth and Ruge demanded that the mentally challenged teenager's brother give them a huge pig in compensation for the alleged arson scandalized Margaret. "Toby's wife worked hard to raise that pig and was going to kill it and give the cooked meat to all those who had paid her bride price. Even you, in return for the cash you contributed." Margaret was wise enough, however, to play along with the charade. Ruge and his three wives did much for the village and were the primary sponsors of the *singsing* that heralded Ruge's leadership in the upcoming pig kill. The fire had destroyed Elizabeth's trade store and money she had stored under her bed for that bid. Still, Margaret remained unconvinced by Elizabeth's spin on events, later joining others in condemning the cruel turn that ended in Toby's nervous breakdown and his family forced to flee Yandera for their distant gardens.

When a dog died howling under my house one day, I was interviewing several women about child rearing. Startled by the piercing cry, we rushed outside. The emaciated dog was already stiffening in a grotesque posture. Several boys, who had come out of the nearby schoolhouse, moved the dead dog out from under my raised house. And Margaret offered to find something – banana leaves or a piece of old cloth – to cover the dog. Before Margaret could leave the scene, however, one of Ruge's wives, Antonia, suggested that the dog had died as a result of the "poison" emanating from the batteries in my tape recorder! Her eyes wide with concern, another of Ruge's wives, Rosa, predicted that the owner of the dog would demand compensation of me for killing his dog. Translating the distraught women's hysterical *tok ples** for me, Margaret smoothly intervened – in Gende and pidgin English – asserting that the dog had died from heart worm (a common occurrence among the village mongrels) and that I had nothing to do with the its gruesome death.

So the poised and as far as I knew un-superstitious Margaret shocked me one night when she burst into my house with blood gushing from a deep gash on her leg and crying "Ghost! Ghost! I saw a ghost!" Sitting her down on one of my two folding chairs, my hands trembling, I washed her leg with cold water from one of my metal water buckets and cleaned and dressed the wound with antiseptic and bandages. As I did, she told me how she had stayed late on a shopping trip to the mountain across from us, playing cards with some Chimbu people from the other side of the divide between Chimbu and Gende territories. When she finally came down it was already dark. Carrying a container of kerosene for me along with supplies from the well-stocked trade store at Pandambai, Margaret was startled by a white apparition that sprang out of a clump of tall bamboo. Margaret dropped her flashlight, *bilum* and everything else as she stumbled and slid down the mountain, too frightened to scream. An old woman had been buried near there not long before and Margaret was sure it was her ghost that she had seen.

It wasn't until Margaret came into my house that she realized she was bleeding. She apologized several times for leaving our supplies on the mountain even though I said, "It doesn't matter. It doesn't matter." I felt guilty for not having gone with her. I chose instead to stay back in the village writing up field notes – which could have been done anytime. But having made the arduous climb on other occasions, I decided against it this time. Pandambai was over 8000 feet in elevation, much higher than Yandera at 5000 feet. To get to Pandambai, one had to climb down our mountain first, cross the swinging wire bridge (with its missing wooden slats) over the rumbling Tai-Ayor River and then climb a very steep track to get to Pandambai, a 'short-cut' favored by the Gende over the longer dirt road that switched back and forth up the mountain. It was easier to pay Margaret to pick up a few things for me than to go with her, slowing her down and having to endure remarks about how "red-faced white people were when they exerted themselves" or the more forgiving "you grew up in town" or "a flat place." I took consolation in the fact that I was never reduced to being carried across streams and up mountains as some white visitors to Papua New Guinea (including Margaret Mead) had been in the past, the excuse being that they had to preserve their leather shoes.

When I finished taping Margaret's leg, the Coleman lantern I had set beside the chair so that I could better see what I was doing started rocking violently. Both Margaret and I jumped up, Margaret knocking me back as she vaulted for the door, shouting that the ghost had followed her into my house. Thinking it might be an earthquake, I glanced first at the bucket of water and then at the glass container filled with kerosene that was attached to my kerosene stove. Neither liquid was sloshing back and forth as they did when there were tremors, yet the lantern was still rocking. Standing by the open door, I considered running after Margaret as a chill came over me and I thought – for a few seconds – that, maybe, a ghost was indeed in my house. I could hear Margaret in the house behind mine broadcasting the news to Ruge's family and exclaiming excitedly, "I saw a ghost and now it's in Laura's house!"

Grabbing my flashlight, I shut off the lantern. Standing by my open door, in case of what I was not sure, I waited a good fifteen minutes before latching it and going to bed. I zipped myself into my sleeping bag, fully dressed and with the flashlight tucked inside beside me, ready to light up any intruder, living or dead. It was a long time before I fell asleep, mostly because

I wondered why no one had shouted out or come to see if I were okay.

The next day, Margaret showed up early, sheepishly snickering about running away. She handed me the recovered yellow plastic kerosene container. I asked her, "Why did you leave me alone last night? I was frightened, too. I barely slept."

Sitting down on the floor and accepting a mug of tea, Margaret scowled disdainfully and replied, "Ghosts don't hurt white people!"

*Translations of Tok Pisin words (pidgin English, a lingua franca spoken throughout Papua New Guinea): 1) *misis* – European, or white woman; 2) *bilum* – string netbag; 3) *singsing* – festival with drumming, songs and dance; 4) *tok ples* –local language

Laura Zimmer-Tamakoshi, PhD, is the author of many scholarly works on her research in Papua New Guinea. Her website www.theanthropoogistinthefield is a world-wide teaching tool. Other accomplishments include: work as visual media review editor for Pacific Studies (1996-2001), and leadership roles in the Association for Social Anthropology in Oceania and Melanesian Interest Group. She taught at UPNG (1986-1990) and was a research associate at the PNG National Research Institute (2006-2013). Reflecting her interest in making anthropology more accessible, Laura is writing a collection of stories based on her first year in New Guinea that includes "The White Woman will Eat You" (2015, Persimmon Tree). Laura returns to PNG often, most recently in 2014.

After Alaska
Thérése Halscheid

for Lisa

She lives in me now, in the north of my chest, where it is all dark, all
  winter --
to my ears will come her voice, then to my eyes, this white woman,
then pathways to the tribe she roamed with, to places inside me
where they are hunting and she is gathering and there, a certain arrow,
and there, a stab of certain pain

then to moments other than these, to nights when my heart is a drum
for her dancing and her movements tell stories, and I feel in her feet
all that was told to me, all that was shared.

When I breathe and the wind blows in a mighty power, my mouth forms
a small opening and she scales the dark throat to leap where
my lip catches the light, that she might sit
and be warmed for awhile --

I felt her once, during an inner storm, as a certain chill ran through,
after my muscles tightened into big cold mountains
that she was arranging my ribs, arching them, same as the shelters
she spoke of, in the icy north of Alaska, where they shape
whalebone over driftwood and pack it with sod.

There is a veined landscape she traverses in the spring
where my blood runs as thawed rivers

and she waits on the sands of myself for the return of the whale,
propped against a white embankment of bones, knees drawn to her chest
as in the way of the Eskimo, at times looking up, reading
the starry pores, the sky of my cloudless skin.

Therése Halscheid's recent book *Frozen Latitudes* (Press 53), won the Eric Hoffer Book Award, HM for Poetry. Other collections include: *Uncommon Geography*, *Without Home*, and a Greatest Hitschapbook award. Poems and lyric essays have appeared in *The Gettysburg Review*, *Tampa Review*, *Crab Orchard Review*, among other journals. Recent awards include first place in Welcome Table Press's 2015 Creative Nonfiction contest. Therése has been writing on the road for several years. Journeys include the Arctic north of Alaska, where she lived with and taught an Eskimo Inupiaq tribe.

World of Gas

Bonnie Jo Campbell

Propane tanks reclined like rows of swollen white bellies behind the chain link, each tank emblazoned with the Pur-Gas smiling cat logo, one of the boss's idiotic conceptions – he'd apparently forgotten that the "p-u-r" was meant to be pronounced "pure." At the tire-repair shop next door, the compressors rattled and droned, and if the noise didn't actually kill brain cells, then it certainly prevented anyone in the vicinity from thinking clearly. As the Pur-Gas office manager, Susan, talked on the workroom phone, she noticed that she was wadding up her lunch bag so tightly that her knuckles were white. According to the vice principal on the other end of the phone, her oldest son, Josh, was being kicked out of school for fighting.

"Give him some kind of in-school suspension," Susan said. "Otherwise he's going to sit home watching TV all day. He should be learning something."

The vice principal said, "We don't have the personnel to monitor problem students all day."

"Well, I'm at work all day. I can't watch him."

"What about his father?"

"What *about* his father?"

"Somebody's asking you," whispered Darcy, Susan's assistant. Darcy crossed her eyes and signaled "nutcase" by tracing a little circle in the air.

"We'll see what we can do," said the vice principal, sounding annoyed.

"Yeah, thanks a lot." Susan hung up the phone, tossed her lunch bag into the garbage can and returned to the front counter, where she found her brother-in-law Mack, dressed as usual in a camouflage jacket and army cap. For the benefit of her sister Holly and their two kids, Susan always gave Mack her employee's discount. Susan retrieved his paperwork from a file under Holly's name.

"You're sure that's the biggest one I can get?" Mack asked.

"This is a three-thousand-cubic-foot tank, Mack. It's half as big as your trailer. Try not to let any of your drunk buddies drive a truck into it." Propane was apparently the fuel of choice this month for the Y2K crowd, whose members all thought that the flow of natural gas would be compromised at the stroke of midnight December 31, 1999, along with civilization as they knew it.

Mack and his militia pals were by no means the only pain-in-the-ass alarmists in town these days. Susan had ordered survival appliances for fidgeting paper-company executives, two city council members, and last week, the very vice principal with whom she'd just been speaking – maybe she should call him back and threaten to lose his order for the super-efficient, lightweight propane heat source if he didn't keep Josh at school. All these men thought that the big collapse was coming, and they were cocksure enough to think that through clever planning and by purchasing the right machines they would survive, huddling in their basements or manning their guard towers.

"Them delivery trucks run on propane or gasoline?" asked Mack, who was not a bad-looking guy when he wasn't done up like an idiot commando.

"Propane."

"Good. That means the trucks'll have fuel to make deliveries."

"Don't worry, the trucks'll be running."

It occurred to Susan that men were always waiting for something cataclysmic – love or war or a giant asteroid. Every man wanted to be a hot-heated Bruce Willis character, fighting against the evil foreign enemy while despising the domestic bureaucracy. Men wanted to focus on jus one big thing, leaving the thousands of smaller messes for the women around them to clean up.

"You're too negative, too cynical," Susan's husband (now ex-husband) has told her. "And you don't love me the way you used to. That's why I had to find somebody else."

"Tell it to your kids," Susan had said. "Tell it to Josh and Andy and Tommy."

Men didn't understand that you couldn't let yourself be consumed with passion when there were so many people needing your attention, when there was so much work to do. Men didn't understand that there was nothing big enough to exempt you from your obligations, which began as soon as the sun rose over the paper company and ended only after you'd finished the day's chores and fell exhausted into sleep against the background nose of I-94.

This millennium business was just another distraction to keep men from being of any goddamned use whatsoever. Instead of going to all this fuss and expense, Mack ought to hire a babysitter once a week and take Holly out for dinner or maybe clean up the yard around their trailer, which, last time Susan saw it, was littered with motor-oil bottles, rotting lumber, and automobile engines covered with tarps. And now that he was preparing for Y2K, Mack has gotten hold of a 550-gallon diesel tank that lay like a big yellow turd under Holly's clotheslines. Apparently Mack was going to fill the tank with fuel for this truck.

"You've got to have a four-inch concrete pad for this propane tank," Susan said. "We're going to have to come out to inspect it before you pour, and after."

"I'm pouring the slab tomorrow." From his pocket, Mack produced some papers. With great seriousness, he said, "Susan, I know we haven't always gotten along, but you ought to have a copy of this," and he unfolded a four-page stapled packet of instructions for Y2K preparation. Susan stopped writing and read to herself randomly form the back page: "Fill your bathtub with water," and "Have a minimum of a thousand rounds of ammunition for every gun you own." The noise of the compressors next door seemed to intensify, and the men shouted and dropped tools onto the concrete floor. As usual, the radio out back was turned to the Rush Limbaugh station.

Susan looked into Mack's squinting face, wadded the pages into a ball, and tossed it over the counter, missing the can behind him by three feet. "None of you sons a bitches get it, do you?" Susan's voice grew loud. "If the power goes out, we'll all just have to live without power for a while. Whatever happens, happens. You can't control the world, and you especially can't control this propane!" Susan's voice rose to a crescendo, and Darcy looked in from around the corner, a cheese and meat sandwich falling open in her hand. Susan resumed at a whisper, "You know, if I tell the driver not to fill your tank, he won't fill it. So you'd better be good to Holly."

Mack moved away from the counter and studied his black army boots. Susan marked three places on the form where Mack had to sign and held out a pen. In a businesslike voice she said, "If you don't use a hundred dollars a month worth of this gas, you'll have to pay double rent on the tank."

That afternoon, Susan skipped swimming at the Y and went right home. Before even going into the kitchen, she followed the stairs down to the basement into which Josh, two months ago, had moved his bedroom. That had allowed Andy and Tommy to have their own rooms.

"Josh?" She tapped on the door to what used to be her husband's office, but there was no answer. She pushed the door open into a room lit only by the bluish glow of the television.

"You're home early, Mom!" Josh shouted in an accusatory tone.

"Josh, I got a call – " Susan stopped talking as soon as she realized there were two bodies in Josh's bed. "Nicole?" Josh's latest curly-haired girlfriend was with him, the sheet pulled up to her neck. As Susan's eyes adjusted, she realized Josh was naked. For Christ's sake, they were fifteen years old! Susan was struck dumb, listening, despite herself, to the intonations of surprise and anger emanating from what appeared to be *The Jerry Springer Show*. Finally, Susan yelled, "Get up!"

"I don't just come into your room," Josh said.

"Get up!" Susan stepped outside the door, crossed her arms over her chest, and tried to think of what to say. The girl came out first, with mascara smeared around her eyes. She looked at Susan defiantly before heading to the stairs; the girls' face was so pale and thin that Susan wondered if she could be one of those girls who threw up her food.

"I love her, Mom," Josh said. "You wouldn't understand that." Susan noticed that Josh's face was sprouting not just peach fuzz, but also a few wiry, dark hairs.

"Well, if you love her, then why in the hell would you take a chance on getting her pregnant?" asked Susan. "Why take a chance on screwing up both your lives?" Susan was also thinking: if this girl means so much to you, the why don't you turn off the damned TV when you're in bed with her?

Dishwashing was Susan's last chore before going to bed that night. The hot water was making her sleepy, and she let herself forget about Josh and think about Y2K. She'd been so busy scoffing at the alarmists that she hadn't let herself really think about the year 2000. She understood the principle involved with the zero-zero date and that it could cause problems with computer systems controlling traffic lights and ATM machines. Maybe she'd allow extra time to get to work on Monday, January 3. Maybe she ought to have a couple hundred dollars on hand in case her first paycheck was screwed up. She could easily fill her bathtub with water, but probably she wouldn't bother. Although her bastard of an ex-husband called her negative and cynical, she truly believed that regular people doing their jobs could fix whatever problems resulted from the glitch.

Susan opened the window to allow a stream of cold night air into the room, and she listened to the hum of traffic from the highway, the buzz of an airplane flying over, the muted din of third-shift work at the paper factory, and the sound of the TV blathering in the basement. Josh would be lying in his bed, passed out with his mouth open when she went down to turn it off. When Susan pressed the power button, he'd complain, half-asleep," "I was watching that, Mom." She knew she hadn't said the right things to him about Nicole earlier, and she was still too pissed off to know what she should say.

Susan submerged her hands in the warm water again. She could see some advantages to a real millennium breakdown. Life would be quieter without power. She imagined the hands of her kitchen clock spinning faster and faster, racing toward New Year's Eve, and then stopping. At the critical moment, she'd be standing at the sink like this, maybe burning a balsam-scented Christmas-tree candle on the windowsill. She'd be exhausted from her father's visit; he always came December 24th and stayed until New Year's Eve, which meant she had to keep the house clean all week and get up early to cook hot breakfasts for him – the man thought the world would end if they didn't all sit down to a cooked breakfast. Suddenly smoke would cease to flow from the paper-company stacks. The lights would all go out, and the factory's whirling, rattling, clanking machines would fall silent. Susan would dry her hands and put on some hand lotion and exhale deeply. In Susan's millennium moment, even the headlights of the delivery trucks would dim and die as wheels stopped turning. On all lanes of the highway, four wheel-drive vehicles and ordinary cars would grind to a halt, along with their drivers. Overhead, the stars would shine as brightly as they did in the desert sky. Men revving motorcycles, chain saws, and lawn tractors in garages would wind down, too, their machines becoming dead, oiled metal in their hands. The voices of vice principals, men who ordered Pur-Gas, and guys jabbering on TV and radio would slow and then stop, if only for a moment. Men of all ages everywhere – men talking about football, auto engines, politics, hydraulic pumps, and the mechanics of love – would finally just shut up.

Bonnie Jo Campbell is author of the best-selling novel *Once Upon A River* (2011, W.W. Norton) and a Guggenheim Fellow. Her new story collection is *Mothers, Tell Your Daughters* (October 2015, W.W. Norton). In 2009, she was a National Book Award and National Book Critics Circle Award finalist for *American Salvage*, which won the Foreword Book of the Year Award for Short Fiction. Earlier works include the novel, *Q Road* and the story collection *Women and Other Animals*. Her poetry collection *Love Letters to Sons of Bitches* won the 2009 CBA Letterpress Chapbook Award. She's received the AWP Award for Short Fiction, a Pushcart Prize, and the Eudora Welty Prize. Campbell teaches in the Low Residency Program at Pacific University and lives in Kalamazoo. www.bonniejocampbell.com.

Afterward

Maintaining and Operating a Small Press was first offered as a theoretical class in which students created a business plan for their hypothetical independent presses. Students learned about profit & loss statements, developed a mission, formulated a plan for getting authors, and created potential marketing plans based on made-up books they would publish. There was a great deal of knowledge they could take with them to a potential job, however, long-lasting learning takes place when it moves from the hypothetical to a tangible project.

With deep thanks to PS Books, this is the second year in which students have stepped away from the abstract and worked in a setting to take a book from conception to publication. My goal was not to lecture or tell the students how to publish the book but rather serve as a resource. To achieve the end goal – the students were divided into four teams: Business, Editorial, Design & Layout, and Marketing & Sales. Each student served as a team co-chair and then served as a worker on two other teams.

Every week we met to discuss the status for each team. The lack of formal structure, where I would lecture and students would then respond with some action, caused some initial frustration. Students were put in real-world situations, which forced them to think, problem-solve, and respond. As a class, we discussed blunders and mistakes: how they could be prevented, how to respond, and how to recover. The value in being able to make a mistake without the threat of losing one's job, is immeasurable.

This has been an incredibly challenging and rewarding experience for all involved. I know each student will look back on this class with a great sense of accomplishment, not only for their hard work, but also because they helped bring this anthology to life.

Best wishes,
Anne Converse Willkomm, MFA '10
Director of the Graduate Publishing Program

Permissions

Grateful acknowledgment is made to the following for permission to re-print previously published material:

Robin Black: "Let Nothing Ye Dismay or the Eternal Self-Hatred of the Abused Child's Mind," copyright © 2014 by Robin Black. First appeared in *The Rumpus*.

Tori Bond: "Happy Anniversary," copyright © 2013 by Tori Bond. First appeared in *The Bicycle Review Online*.

Frances Boyle: "Rest Cure," copyright © 2011 by Frances Boyle. First appeared in *This Magazine Online*.

Laura J. Bobrow: "An Ordinary Housewife," copyright © 2015 by Laura J. Bobrow. First appeared in the collection *Betrayed*, published by Finishing Line Press.

Mara Buck: "Short Order, Long Time," copyright © 2015 by Mara Buck. First appeared in *The Tishman Review*.

Vickie A. Carr: "Revlon Shade No. 37," copyright © 1990 by: Vickie A. Carr. First appeared in *The Widener Review*.

Robin Rosen Chang: "Empathy," copyright © 2014 by Robin Rosen Chang. First appeared in *WomenArts Quarterly*.

Denise Clemons: "Dad-isms," copyright © 2009 by Denise Clemons. First appeared in *Relationships And Other Stuff*, published by Natasha Brooks.

C.A. Cole: "Down the Back of an Eagle," copyright © 2012 by C.A. Cole. First appeared in *Granny Smith Magazine*.

J.V. Foerster: "Apple Girl," copyright © 2011 by J.V. Foerster. First appeared in *Fox Chase Review*.

Tery Aine Griffin: "Blue Smell of Steel," copyright © 1991 by Tery Aine Griffin. First appeared in *The Wittenberg Review*.

Therese Halscheid: "After Alaska," copyright © 2008 by Therese Halscheid. First appeared in *The Connecticut Review*.

Lisa Lawmaster Hess: "Casting the First Stone," copyright © 2014 by Lisa Lawmaster Hess. First appeared in the novel *Casting the First Stone*, published by Lighthouse Publishing of the Carolinas. Reprinted with permission of Lighthouse Publishing of the Carolinas.

Alison Hicks: "The Mother as Persephone," copyright © 2014 by Alison Hicks. First appeared as "The Daughter as Persephone" in *Storyscape*.

Alison Jaenicke: "Freefall," copyright © 2014 by Alison Jaenicke. First appeared in *Superstition Review*.

Andrea Jarrell: "The Getaway," copyright © 2014 by Andrea Jarrell. First appeared in *Full Grown People*.

Anne Kaier: "Bone-House," copyright © 2014 by Anne Kaier. First appeared in *Referential Magazine*.

Miriam N. Kotzin: "Sugar Ants," copyright © 2012 by Miriam N. Kotzin. First appeared in *Flashquake*.

Dawn Lowe: "Beyond Polite Conversation," copyright © 2013 by Dawn Lowe. First appeared in the collection *Parent of Suicide: A Year of Creative Writing*, printed by CreateSpace.

Grace Marcus: "Grove of the Patriarchs," copyright © 2010 by Grace Marcus. First appeared in *Philadelphia Stories*.

Deborah Miller-Collins: "Facebook Lies," copyright © 2015 by Deborah Miller-Collins. First appeared in *Empty Sink Publishing*.

Elizabeth Mosier: "Animator," copyright © 2015 by Elizabeth Mosier. First appeared in *Harpers Ferry Review Online*.

J.D. Munro: "Life Cycles," copyright ©2013 by J.D. Munro. First appeared in *Gulf Coast*.

Rachel Pastan: "Leaving," copyright © 2014 by Rachel Pastan. First appeared as "Three Windows" in *Fifth Wednesday Journal*.

Tina Pisco: "Aller Simple," copyright © 2010 by Tina Pisco. First appeared in the collection *She Be*, published by Bradshaw Books.

Gail Priest: "Annie Crow Knoll: Sunset," copyright © 2014. First appeared in the novel *Annie Crown Knoll: Sunset*, published by Hayson Publishing.

Peg Alford Pursell: "Day of the Dead," copyright © 2013 by Peg Alford Pursell. First appeared in *The Quotable*.

Susan Blackwell Ramsey: "The Year Hits Perimenopause," copyright © 2012 by Susan Blackwell Ramsey. First appeared in the collection *A Mind Like This*, published by University of Nebraska Press.

Cynthia Reeves: "The Punk Test," copyright © 2014 by: Cynthia Reeves. First appeared in the collection *Wreckage of Reason II: Back To The Drawing Board*, published by Spuyten Duyvil Press.

Dorothy Ryan: "A Gala Occasion," copyright © 2002 by Dorothy Ryan, First appeared in the collection *To Love One Another: Poems Celebrating Marriage*, published by Grayson Books.

C.J. Spataro: "Bent and Blue," copyright © 2006 by Carla Spataro. First appeared in *XConnect: Writers of the Information Age*.

Elaine Terranova: "Awake," copyright © 2015 by Elaine Terranova. First appeared in *Hotel Amerika*.

J.C. Todd: "Men Kissing," copyright © 1994 by J.C. Todd. First appeared in *The Paris Review*.

Megan Vered: "Amen," copyright © 2014 by Megan Vered. First appeared in *The Penman Review*.

Susan Weaver: "Last Walk with My Sister," copyright © 2014 by Susan Weaver. First appeared in *Schuylkill Valley Journal*.

Anne Willkomm: "Albee," copyright © 2012 by Anne Willkomm. First appeared in *Midwest Coast Review*.

"World of Gas" reprinted from *American Salvage* by Bonnie Jo Campbell. Copyright © 2009 Wayne State University Press, with the permission of Wayne State University Press.

Laura Zimmer-Tamakoshi: "The White Woman will Eat You!" copyright © 2015 by Laura Zimmer-Tamakoshi. First appeared in *Permission Tree: An Online Magazine of the Arts by Women Over Sixty*.